HOW
TO HAVE A WELL-MANNERED
DOG

In the same series.

Choose and Bring up Your Puppy, *By Kay White*
The Right Way to Keep Dogs
The Right Way to Keep Cats
The Right Way to Keep Ponies
The Right Way to Keep Pet Fish
The Right Way to Keep Rabbits
The Right Way to Keep Pet Birds
The Right Way to Keep Hamsters

All uniform with this book

How To Have A
WELL-MANNERED
DOG

by

KAY WHITE

and

J. M. EVANS, M.R.C.V.S.

Pictures by Harold White

PAPERFRONTS

**ELLIOT RIGHT WAY BOOKS
KINGSWOOD, SURREY, U.K.**

Every effort is made to ensure that Paperfronts and Right Way Books are accurate, and that the information given in them is correct. However, information can become out of date, and author's or printers' errors can creep in. This book is sold, therefore, on the condition that neither Author nor Publisher can be held legally responsible for the consequences of any error or omission there may be.

Made and Printed in Great Britain by Hunt Barnard Printing Ltd., Aylesbury, Bucks.

CONTENTS

Resisting Temptation!
Lavish praise and a delicious food reward should be given.

ILLUSTRATIONS

DEDICATION.

To Anna the Doberman, and Tigger, Pooka and Berry the Boxers, and

ALL GOOD DOGS!

ACKNOWLEDGEMENTS.

Our grateful thanks for specialist help go to Mrs Jackie White, of Eastbourne, Sussex, who knows about babies as well as dogs, and to Harold White, co-owner of the Boxers, who drew the pictures and worked out the charts so cleverly.

Our gratitude and admiration also goes to the animal behaviourists on both sides of the Atlantic on whose experience we have drawn, particularly Dr Victoria Voith, Dr William E Campbell, Dr Peter J Volmer, Dr Roger Mugford and Dr Michael Fox.

INTRODUCTION

FOR thousands of years we have been content to have dogs as our companions, to admire them, love them, perhaps even rely on them, but until recently we have not been able to study the way a dog's mind works, the way it learns, and the way it interprets the actions of human beings.

Small wonder that well-meaning people and well-intentioned dogs sometimes find themselves at cross-purposes. Because our world is getting to be a more difficult place in which to keep pets, it is not possible to be tolerant of badly behaved pets as it was fifty years ago. We owe it to our fellow citizens to make sure that our pets cause them no annoyance; dogs must not become a bone of contention between neighbours.

It is fortunate that we now have the benefit of studies, originally made in the United States and now going on in many other countries, into the natural behaviour patterns of dogs and their responses to human beings. The work of these animal behaviourists and years of experience with our own dogs has provided the knowledge that makes it possible to bring up puppies to be fun-loving but well behaved members of the family group without the need for harsh, formal training.

We do not speak of *training* puppies but of *managing* them so that the puppy learns what is acceptable and unacceptable behaviour from the time it enters your home. We believe that if you follow the advice in this book, your new puppy will have much less chance of acquiring bad habits and you will be in the happy position of seldom having to punish by physical force the puppy you love.

Doubtless some readers will already own dogs which have acquired annoying, frustrating and even dangerous habits and we believe that if you follow our methods of behaviour control you can turn such an animal into a pet, a dog which will feel secure and contented about its

9

own life and will consequently be an enrichment to your environment. Dogs need and value their owner's approval very much and we hope to put you and your dog on the same wavelength so that you may communicate easily and be happy together.

Dog management our way does not take a lot of time; you do not necessarily have to go to classes or learn that stamping-shouting-guard drill used in competitions. The secret is all a matter of approaching the dog, puppy or adult, in the right way, and programming your pet to fit in with your way of life. Our management programme starts early, we hope that it will have been begun by the breeder even before the litter is born, but you can begin when you choose your puppy, or when you take it into your home, or even, although this is harder work, you can begin with a dog that already has behaviour problems.

A great deal of reproach is heaped on those people who buy puppies and then discard them to rescue homes or perhaps cruelly abandon them. Sometimes people do not value animal life enough, but we know that in many other cases a lot of mental anguish has been gone through before a decision has to be reached that a certain dog has become unfit to be a companion animal. Just as there are people with intolerable personality defects, so, very occasionally, there are dogs which were born that way or have been made that way by what has happened to them. We cannot help those dogs or their owners, but we know that we can do a great deal for the vast majority of dogs born with sane balanced mental attitudes, but which have picked up bad habits. We hope that the end result will be that far fewer dogs will have to be destroyed as unwanted.

This book is written by two authors, who between them have a comprehensive knowledge of the world of dogs. One, J. M. Evans, is a veterinary surgeon, the other, Kay White, is a dog breeder and kennel owner with a long experience of living with her own and other people's dogs.

This book does not set out to teach you how to train your dog for the gun, or even to do a series of tricks. What it will do is help you to understand your dog, and to act in such a way that your dog can understand you. From there, the whole world of dog ability is open to you, or you may just settle for happy companionship with a well-behaved dog that is the envy of all your friends.

If you already have a dog which has learnt that being a nuisance brings its own rewards, then we will hope to show you that clever remedial work will bring you a dog good as new to enjoy. We say that our methods are clever, because all human beings have more brain power than any dog, and by using our superior intellect we can out-think dogs and make them respect us, electing us the pack leader. Dogs need to know where they fit into a household and what is required of them. They need consistent management to give them a feeling of security in the environment in which they live.

Your commitment in taking on a dog includes the duty to feed, groom, take it to a veterinary surgeon when it is ill, and to make sure it has protective vaccinations. You also take on the obligation to make the dog part of your family until the end of its days. It is a sad aspect of modern society that people often seek to shed the commitment they have made to an animal, but feel sure that someone else will be able to "give it a good home". The pathetic dogs in rescue homes are *people failures*, the victims of people who did not keep their promises, spoken or unspoken, to care for the dog for ever, including teaching it to be an acceptable animal for today's world. It is a rare thing indeed for a dog to fail to keep its unspoken promise of devotion to its owner and its owner's immediate family.

Owning a dog is one of the great pleasures of life, mainly because the dog takes up the slack where human companionship, collaboration and devotion fall short. Dogs give unconditional trust and affection, they are uncritical of our failings and they give the same rapturous welcome always without reproach regardless of our shortcomings. Dogs take years off your age, by providing a compelling reason to take outdoor exercise and also by allowing us to play in a child-like way without looking silly . . . dogs make the ideal excuse!

Dog ownership brings you instant membership of a club which takes in 50% of the population . . . the password is

DOG. With your dog you may nod, smile, even speak to people and receive their cordiality in return in a way that is impossible to non-dog owners.

Patting your dog, and complimenting you on how well behaved it is, may be the only conversational exchange in the day for a lonely person, perhaps now deprived of dog ownership.

The dog is a safety valve in many relationships, sometimes the only bridge across which people can communicate. For only or lonely children, the warm, cuddly responsive dog can be anything the imagination allows, from a magic animal with supernatural powers to a confidant, an agile and enthusiastic playmate, a loyal companion to share the burden of naughtiness, a friend that licks and never tells, or a possession to boast about, a status symbol for a child or a person where enhancement of their own rank is needed.

Wanting a puppy is the most natural instinct in the world; man has been doing just that since before recorded time when dogs became the first domesticated animals.

It was not long after the first man/dog friendships were formed that man realised that dog had a range of talents which could be put to good use. Very soon, fast-running dogs were being bred together to provide offspring which would excel at chasing gazelle and deer. Dogs with long noses and wide nostrils proved good at following scent and they helped track down game. Big dogs with heavy shoulders could pull carts, little dogs with flexible bodies could flush rodents out of holes, dogs that were possessive about their kill could be taught to guard their master's property too. Down the centuries, dogs were specially selected and bred together for their working ability, and those that did not make the grade became pets for children.

The body shape and the fur covering of the dog has been manipulated as no other animal's has been. Sometimes the new breeds of dog were introduced to be specially suitable for a purpose, sometimes just to fill the eye with an object of beauty, sometimes, as in the case of the regional terriers, just for the sake of having something different from the next town, or the next district.

The cult of specialist designed dogs reached its peak at the end of the nineteenth century when breeds which we know so well today, like the Boxer, the Doberman, the Yorkshire Terrier, and the Boston Terrier were deliberately evolved from other canine "ingredients". The dog designers wanted character traits as well as body shape and they planned the ancestry to provide both aspects in the dog they created. We may no longer want the working ability which was built into the dog, but we have to realise that we cannot avoid taking the inborn character as a package deal with the body shape we admire.

We can select away from the character and behaviour trait we want least. The same inbuilt ability and character trends are present in the crossbred and the mongrel, only there you have more of the lucky dip situation in that you may not know the ingredients of the pudding, or the ingredients may never have been compatible. Some crosses seem to produce conflict within the dog itself, for instance, a gundog/guard dog cross (Labrador and Boxer), has proved generally unsuccessful in any role.

The twentieth century has not proved to be a good one for dogs. In the last eighty years, their world has changed even more than our own. Dogs can no longer be allowed their freedom, the motor car has changed all that; dogs are unwelcome in many parts of our intensely farmed countryside. Dogs have had to learn to live in small houses with busy people who cannot always give them all the time and attention which the dog would like and needs. Smaller, one or two generation families mean that dogs have to be alone quite a lot, and they seldom have the opportunity to consort with their own kind, they can never roam the streets in a pack following their own inclinations. Many dogs will never in the whole of their lives experience the exhilaration of doing the work which they know they should be doing and are still capable of doing.

Section I

THE DOG, ITS NATURE AND HABITS

I
THE PACK

WE keep the dogs which we want so much virtually in semi-detached prisons, often in great comfort but to a large extent our dogs are frustrated, bored and idle. We might ourselves find it very difficult to be happy if we were shut in a luxury hotel with no occupation for virtually twenty-four hours a day, with nothing to anticipate but meal breaks. Dogs, ever adaptable, are learning very quickly to fit in. They do not mind very much being out of work although when an opportunity to follow their old occupation comes up, they find it hard to resist. The inborn instinct to dig, to chase or to fight or to bid for pack leadership can rise to the surface at inappropriate times.

Our world in the 1980s demands that dogs assume a subordinate role. You cannot as an owner take a pride in a dog which is a nuisance to itself and others. You have a duty not to allow the dog that is part of your life to spoil the enjoyment of others who have chosen not to have a dog.

Although dogs have been domesticated to a degree for so long, they have never been so totally domestic as now, when the majority of dogs are kept only for companionship. Even more frustrating is the life style demanded of the gundog which accompanies its owner perhaps only once a week . . . the days between must seem very long and the dog has to adjust to boredom alternated with activity. Every new puppy has to learn to fit into the home into which it is taken, to fit in with the ways of its new owners, to be what they want it to be. We feel we can show you how to help your puppy to adapt and to achieve a happy dog/owner relationship in a much more subtle way than the somewhat aggressive *training* so often advocated.

In order to "manage" your puppy properly it is important to understand the nature of dogs, the way they think and communicate both to people and to other dogs, and the way their natural wild society would be ordered.

Dogs in the wild are essentially pack animals. The pack works together to find and kill food, to protect each other by warning of the approach of an enemy. Pack members will bring up each other's young and to a certain extent they will look after the sick and the weak. Their strength is that of a group working for the benefit of the whole. This group strength still survives in hunting packs of foxhounds and beagles which have a communal brain and a communal ability but often not too much individual intellect.

The survival of the wild dog packs depended on a ranking order with one male and one female taking dominant leader roles and the rest establishing themselves in descending order of status, each subordinate to the ones above in the pack. Continual bids for leadership will be made, just as in human society. When the pack leaders are young and strong their dominant role is maintained, but with age and infirmity the pack leader would either be killed in a fight or replaced by a challenger. Where several dogs are kept together in a domestic situation, the elderly pack leader seems to withdraw in old age and allow another strong character to take over authority. Some pack members are not ambitious and never seek to raise their status, others spend their lives trying to improve their position and seeking confrontation with the pack leader.

Every litter born to every bitch is essentially a dog pack from the time of the birth. At first dominance is by strength only, the more virile puppies seeking out and holding on to the most productive teats, but as the puppies gain ability, the guile, courage, agility and a spirit of adventure begin to show in the potential pack leader.

The middle ranks follow with middling ability and there are always placid unambitious individuals, and always an under-dog, shy, retiring, perhaps bullied by the others from as young as three weeks old. All the puppies, even the most pushy ones are subordinate to their mother. Even if she is herself a low ranking dog in a kennel situation, she assumes the place of pack leader to her puppies. From the time of their birth she is the source of food, warmth and comfort for them, they depend on her in their early weeks for the stimulating licking and body massage which triggers elimination in the very young puppy. Later the bitch will give her puppies life experience as she plays with them, simulating a fight and being perhaps a little rough, but then giving the puppies the opportunity to attack her. It is very obviously a learning environment in which the puppies find out what it is like to be attacked and to be at the mercy of a stronger animal, and is quite fascinating to watch but is not often seen by visitors to a kennel.

The bitch is very strongly protective to her puppies in the first days after their birth, it is with some reluctance that she leaves them for even a few minutes. The breeder should ensure that the bitch and puppies are kept in a secluded place at this time, because if the bitch feels vulnerable, this can be communicated to the puppies and make them nervous. The bitch fears attack from other dogs, and perhaps cats, but she also resents visits from strange people; the most domesticated pet becomes close to the primitive dog at this time and her primary need is to keep her litter a secret so that they cannot be killed by predators. It is not unknown for other bitches to kill a litter, so there is still adequate reason for the bitch's behaviour.

Gradually, the bitch relaxes protection of the puppies until at about three weeks after the birth, they come to the beginning of the socialisation period when the litter should be brought out of seclusion and given every opportunity to see people and hear household noises, because it is at this time that they begin to adjust to the human world in which they have to live, although the maximum socialisation period does not begin until the puppies are six weeks old.

Orphan puppies which have been bottle reared lack the schooling which teaches them to behave properly with other dogs. This may not matter if they are always to live protected pet lives, but it is important in big breeds or in dogs which you hope will take part in activities with other dogs. Orphan puppies may lack the urge to mate with their own kind and they may be desperately unhappy if put into boarding kennels.

The attitude of the bitch to her puppies is the keynote of your plan for diplomatic dog management. As the puppies pass from the almost totally helpless, blind, deaf state in which they were born to seeing, hearing, running and barking animals at 3–4 weeks old, the bitch begins to teach the puppies the rules for life with her. Still the kind and loving mother, she very definitely indicates that there are some things she will not tolerate. It may be stealing her food, biting her ears, or using her head to play "climbing Everest" when she and the rest of the litter want to sleep. When a puppy is annoying the bitch she acts instantly . . . either by picking it up by the scruff of the neck, or by snapping at the air close to its ear, perhaps with a little rumbly growl as a first warning. The puppy, taken by surprise, will be startled and may scream, but it is unlikely to be physically hurt. The puppy usually runs, or crawls away to think the situation over . . . and whether it runs or crawls may be a pointer to its future character. It may approach and repeat the annoying behaviour, and the "bitch treatment" will be repeated as often as it takes to bring home to the puppy "the action you are doing is against my rules and I AM IN CHARGE HERE."

When the puppy returns to the bitch in a different frame of mind, the puppy is lovingly received, washed and comforted. No grudges are born and there is no nagging. Punishment is applied as the offending act is committed, never afterwards when the puppy has forgotten what it did, and forgiveness and restitution of care and benevolence is apparent as soon as the puppy's attitude alters. This is the right treatment for the very young, although later on, it may pay to cold shoulder or ignore an older puppy for longer to reinforce the notion that bad behaviour results in being an outcast from the pack. Copy the bitch in managing your puppy, particularly when it is young and you will not be far wrong, but "bitch style" means that you must be constantly with the puppy during its early weeks in your home.

You cannot bring up a puppy correctly from a distance,

and you cannot expect a puppy to learn if there is no-one available to teach it and to correct unacceptable behaviour as it occurs.

The Puppy Pack

The way the breeder manages the litter from birth, or even before birth, is important to the eventual purchasers of the puppies. Most pedigree dog breeding is orientated towards each litter producing one or more successful show winners, and so the breeder's aim is physical beauty plus health. While temperament is said to be a consideration, we have to admit that unless temperament is extremely bad (dog bites the judge), it is not a quality that is examined in the show ring. We also must take into consideration that breeders are very used to managing dogs, and their homes are usually run to give the dogs priority. What may seem to the breeder a dog of good temperament may not prove to be so in a companion dog, but most breeders today take great care to interview puppy buyers quite exhaustively, so that they have a very good idea whether the dog they breed will fit into a particular home and be what the new owner wishes it to be.

The majority of puppies in the majority of breeds are sensible and well-balanced, and capable of over-riding a bad early experience and adjusting to less than expert handling in their first home. There is a close parallel to the bringing up of children . . . not many of our parents took a course in child psychology and we all suffered a bit of unwise, perhaps unjust domination, but we mostly grew up without too many scars. Puppies are much the same, but a wise beginning is a great help to the inexperienced owner.

Puppies get their first taste of the world from their mother, and if she is nervous, then they will learn that the world, or some aspect of it has to be feared. Almost certainly, the quality of fear is a learned behaviour, but it can be learnt very early in life. Fear can also be *unlearnt* but it takes time and patience on the part of the owner.

We have said that puppies at three weeks old are entering an important stage when they must be socialised.

If puppies are left in a kennel, away from human contact and sound at this time, they will grow up unmanageable and unfriendly in contrast to the litter that is exposed to a controlled amount of noise, and to handling and human touch and voices in a variety of tones.

It is being found more and more that puppies are best reared in the house, and not in kennel accommodation. It is not always easy to arrange optimum conditions, and to expose the puppies to contact with a number of people while taking precautions against infectious illness which may be brought into the litter. Puppies need a lot of rest and they should not be over-excited, but the breeder must let them have a number of experiences before they leave for their new homes at seven to eight weeks old. There is, it can be seen, considerable skill in raising a litter which will be true to its breed standard and yet conditioned to be a level-headed companion dog.

When a group of puppies begin to play together, domination comes from the puppies which are largest and have most weight. There is a good deal of play fighting which can escalate to displays of real temper from the smaller individuals with leadership ambitions but at this stage lacking the physical capability to win. While fighting, the puppies learn how far they can go and what amount of pain they can inflict before the enemy turns upon them. They learn to control biting and keep play within bounds, all very useful lessons for later life.

Puppies at play should be watched by the breeder, and they should always be under observation at feeding time, so that access to the food dish and opportunity to have possession of a toy can be manipulated so that all puppies who want to participate have an equal chance. Otherwise, the strong-willed but physically smaller puppy, often the leading bitch, can become conditioned to be over-aggressive. Puppies should not have a struggle to survive in any sense of the word, as over-development of the competitive side of their nature can spoil their suitability as a pet.

It follows that the ideal breeder should be at home, with the puppies for the whole day; the parents of the puppies should be of good equable temperament, also used to living in the house and taking part in family life; that the puppies should be raised in the house, so that they have experience of normal house noises. Puppies must be spoken to often, so that they learn to respond to the human voice;

Fig. 1. Puppy play-pen apparatus.
Apparatus in puppy play-pen to give the opportunity to learn skills and to familiarise with objects. Also the opportunity for communal play which is more constructive than tormenting each other. Dominant puppy climbing out.
A Box with several holes to climb through. B Trapeze. C Apple and orange peel, very exciting when first given. D Bucket. E Rope. F Suspended ring. G Tree branch, bark removed. H Soft ball on string. I Fun with an old duster.

they must be regularly and well fed, receive the veterinary attention they need, and they must be gently handled.

It is obviously not possible to have a litter of puppies running free all over the house, so you will normally find them confined in an enclosure. The run they are enclosed in must be large enough to allow the puppies to get well away from their bed to be clean . . . puppies raised in too small a space will be harder to house-train. A large litter, of eight or more puppies will need two runs, so that the larger male puppies do not persecute the smaller ones. Ideally constructive toys are provided so that the puppies can develop bodily skills.

Puppies must never be short of food or drink. Sometimes well meaning people may feel it is their duty to buy a puppy from a litter which has been neglected or suffered some deprivation. Early starvation, before the puppy is three months old, is very difficult to compensate; it has a profound effect on both the physique and the temperament. Leave the rehabilitation of such puppies to people very experienced in dog rearing and start with a puppy which has had every advantage up until selling time. Start with good material and compound it into a splendid companion dog.

The Dog – what it is

1. A pack animal programmed to be submissive to those of higher status and to dominate those weaker than itself.

2. An animal that prefers not to be alone.

3. A dog barks and howls as a rallying call to the pack, a warning of danger, to draw attention to its own needs, or because it is "imprisoned" and hoping for rescue.

4. A dog is a gorge eater, taking usually all food available to it in case there is none tomorrow. Consequently, the dog vomits easily.

5. A dog's instinct leads it to break down barriers between itself and the place it desires to be, agitation lending impetus to destruction sometimes out of all proportion to the apparent strength of the dog.

6. A dog is agile and athletic and needs to work off the energy we feed into it with diets for maximum nutrition.

7. All dogs and bitches, unless neutered, have at some time in their adult life a desire for sexual activity, preferably with the opposite sex. The sexual impulse in males is of widely different urgency, but most bitches have very high libido for a few days during their heat period. The sexual urge at its height will tend to supersede all learned behaviour so owner control and prevention of breaking out and straying must be very strong at this time.

8. What you have never had, you never miss is a true maxim for the male dog's sexual activity. It is a great mistake to allow your companion dog to mate a bitch just once to oblige a friend, or to be in the company of bitches which are in high season. Stud work is best left to professional stud dogs which have a regular supply of bitches coming to them throughout their fertile years.

9. A dog likes comfort, warmth, and needs and responds to physical touch.

10. In the absence of grooming behaviour by its fellow pack and to enable it to be fit to live within our homes, dogs must be regularly groomed by their owners but they do not need bathing more than twice a year unless there is some smelly deposit on the coat.

11. In the absence of work or training for work, a dog needs some activity for its brain, and constructive play is much better than miles of road walking on the lead.

12. A dog has a different type of brain, and less brain capacity than man. It cannot plan ahead. The dog responds to its senses and outside stimuli, particularly those that happen at regular times. The dog has a memory, possibly stimulated by recurrence of scent, or noise.

13. The dog is a creature of routine and habit and it learns easily by repetition.

14. The dog has all the time in the world to observe its owners, and it does so, even when pretending to be asleep. It is thus able to interpret the tiniest expression of human body language which you may be unaware that you make.

15. The dog "talks" to other canines, and to humans by body posture and facial expression . . . (body language). We can communicate better with dogs if we study their body language.

Embarrassment.

Pack leader and submissive dog.
Start of domination routine.

Pack leader makes ritual growl
and clasps subordinate from
above.

Submissive gesture offering
neck for biting.

Anticipation of a reward.

The apprehensive expression.

Fig. 2. Facial expressions and dog body language.
Like those of people, dogs' facial expressions vary. Spend
time observing your own dog.

16. A dog prefers to have its owner's approval; it hates to be at odds with its pack, and especially the pack leader.

17. The dog can experience many of the moods and emotions in the human range. They know anger, pleasure, fright, apprehension and anxiety. They can be full of hope and then disappointed, they may be sad, they feel jealousy keenly. They love deeply, they get lonely, and the absence of one person from the pack can cause deep distress. And they get very, very bored.

2

DOG PROFILES

Things Dogs do Better than Humans
1. Hear sounds at long distance and far higher range.
2. Acquire information by scent trails.
3. They have greater agility than most people, they run faster and climb better; they twist, turn and dodge better, and they can get through surprisingly small holes.
4. Dogs can take a lot of exercise in a short time.
5. They keep a very persistent and constant watch on happenings on their territory and the body movements of their owners.

Things Dogs Cannot Do
1. Think in advance.
2. Interpret *words*; they listen to *sounds* and intonation.
3. Recognition of unfamiliar shapes at long distance; identify by colour.
4. Dogs are not good at deception, treachery, or falsehood.

The Dog is Susceptible to:
1. Pack leadership.
2. Habit, routine.
3. Rewards of many types, especially food and praise.
4. Magic, thrown objects and deterrents which appear to come from outer space.

The Dominant dog stands upright, line of hair on spine (the hackles) stands erect, tail up and gently wagging. This is a primeval device to make the dog look larger and more fierce, and it is caused by the upsurge of adrenalin which precipitates the fight and flight syndrome.

When approached by other dogs, the dominant animal curls its lip, makes a snarling roar, neck is extended, paw may be put on approaching dog.

Submissive dog approaches the other from the side, never head on. Head is held low, body crouching, rear end high. Licks head and lips of pack leader. Finally presents back of neck (vital part) for pack leader to bite, or rolls on its back to expose the groin area. But if submission ritual is well done, there will be no bite inflicted.

Puppies from three to nine months old *expect* to be submissive to adults, even those physically much smaller than themselves. Adult dogs may punish and reprimand puppies but they do not fight them.

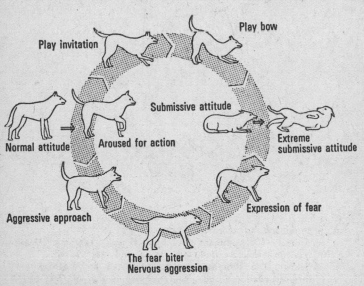

Play bow

Play invitation

Submissive attitude

Normal attitude   Aroused for action

Extreme submissive attitude

Expression of fear

Aggressive approach

The fear biter
Nervous aggression

Fig. 3. Attitudes.

Urination Rituals

Both males and females urinate in the squatting position as puppies. At about nine months to one year old the male will begin urinating with raised leg, this position is more convenient for marking posts and bushes. Territory marking usually goes with the onset of adult behaviour. Bitches

Fig. 4. Dominant and submissive dogs.
   Above: The dominant dog shows signs of aggression, legs straight, hackles raised, tail waving, and teeth bared.
   Below: The submissive smile, which is accompanied by lowered head and body, lowered wagging tail, and may progress to lying on side and exposing the groin.

mark, but at the squat, usually only when coming into season.

Adult males mark their territory and regular walks by directing a stream of urine at certain well defined points, probably endeavouring to blot out the mark of other dogs. Males may also mark, but usually once only, new objects brought into the house, such as a broom or a chair. It may be that these objects have been marked invisibly by a dog in factory or store.

If you have another male dog in house or garden, or a bitch in season nearby, or even a visitor with bitch-scent on their clothes, your own male may feel impelled to mark, even indoors. This behaviour is offensive to us, but so instinctive in the male dog that it is doubtful whether it merits punishment, but it should be discouraged as described later. The remedy is to limit the other dogs visiting the territory and to be sure all marking is completely expunged with some other scent . . . bleach is good where it is possible to use it, without harm to fabrics and carpet. Dogs seem to be able to find a lot of interest in other dogs' fæces; this should be stopped as much as possible to prevent the transmission of infection.

Bitches can be difficult about urination away from home, if they cannot use the same type of surface they are used to; some will only use grass, others concrete. Bitches will hold their urine for up to 48 hours in such circumstances although given every opportunity to be clean. Bitches often behave in this way in boarding kennels, and it is taken as a sign of acceptance of the kennel when at last the bitch will christen her run with a big puddle.

Puppies and emotional bitches may urinate involuntarily in extreme pleasure, perhaps as a greeting; they usually grow out of this habit, which is a demonstration of submission.

Licking

Most dogs lick their feet and genitals to keep them clean. This is a natural act but it should only be allowed for a limited time when necessary. Licking is also a submissive act, but puppies will lick the mouth of a bitch to trigger a regurgitation of partly digested food. This may be the reason that puppies tend to lick children all round the face if they are allowed to. Blood and suppurative discharges are attractive to the dog and they seem impelled to lick wounds.

Sleeping Behaviour

Dogs turn in circles before lying down to flex the spine before going into a tightly curled position to conserve body heat. Only when very warm will they sleep on their sides with feet extended; when a dog is very hot it may lie on its stomach with hind feet extended to bring as much surface as possible in contact with a cool floor. A very relaxed and warm dog will lie on its back with four feet bent up. Dogs will readily assume any position for which they have been extravagantly praised or which has proved rewarding. Our puppy, Berry, looked so appealing lying on her back with feet in the air that we were impelled to pay her attention; now she slides into this pose often, very obviously keeping her eyes on us to see if it has been noticed.

Dogs dream, as people do. They give muffled barks and kick their legs while still deeply asleep.

Vocal Behaviour

Dogs can vary their bark according to what they want to convey. Most dogs bark at doorbells but seldom at telephones. This may be because the owners are not apprehensive of a telephone call. Howling is regarded by many people as a bad omen but to the dog it is just a sound that carries better than a bark, and howling is always done standing or sitting, never on the move, as barking may be. The growl and snarl are warnings of further action to come, unless the adversary gives in. It may be only bluff on the dog's part, but it is up to the owner to see that a dog never ends a growling session as a winner. Some dogs communicate with a grunt-growl noise; be sure which your dog is doing.

Tail wagging means pleasure, but waving the tail may be a sign of aggression. Tails are tucked down between legs when a dog runs away in fear, except in the grey-hound-type dogs which habitually carry their tails in this position. (Borzoi, Italian Greyhound.)

Some dogs, although not of guarding breed, become very possessive about their bed, toys or bones. This attitude must be broken down very early, as the owner must be superior to the dog in every way, even to taking its possessions.

A "biter" is not a guard dog, it is just a dangerous dog. The dog that backs away, snapping and biting through fear is showing its own incompetence at dealing with a situation.

Some dogs show extravagant guarding behaviour when in a car, perhaps because with so much glass around them they feel vulnerable to attack from all sides. Dogs of the guarding breeds should usually be friendly in puppy days; the guard dog instinct often does not show until the dog is two years old.

Stealing

Dogs have no sense of moral values. They take what they find, unless given the direct command, at the time, not to touch. Food should not be left unattended when dogs are present, it is unhygienic to say the least.

3

THE CANINE SENSES

Dogs communicate and get their information about the world by sight, hearing, body language (postures assumed by the body), but mainly by smell. The male dog has a unique sense of territory, and will, when adult, mark with urine several points around the garden and on regular walks, these appear to be sites where he perceives himself to be "in charge". These points are marked again frequently, certainly after any other dog has urinated on the marks he put previously, or if another dog has even passed that way.

It is believed that this urine can vary in strength and

chemical content to convey to other dogs quite a lot about the "marker", including its ferocity and breeding status. Bitches do not perform ritual marking except when coming into season, but some older, dominant bitches will make an attempt at leg raising while urinating . . . probably an excess of masculine component in their personality.

The scenting power of the dog is beyond our comprehension; even the short-nosed dogs can find and identify scent of which we are not even aware. Those dogs with long noses and wide nostrils, and heavy ears bringing the nose close to the ground (Bassets, Bloodhounds) have scenting ability which is almost limitless compared with the human.

The dog's own scent, emitted chiefly from glands under the tail, tells another dog about its temper, intentions and even its pack status. Scent perception makes it difficult for us to deceive or trick dogs; they recognise the clothes we wear for different activities by scent, not colour or fashion design, and they can recognise their owner in any disguise. Dogs will chew on an object just handled by their owner, this is why it is the new book or today's newspaper that get torn and not something discarded days ago. Guard dogs seem to recognise people with bad intentions by the scent they give off, probably the sweat of fear. Puppies find their way to the bitch while they are yet blind and deaf, by scent; the bitch recognises her own newborn puppies by their scent, and will reject any others put into her nest unless the scent of her own litter is applied to them. This special litter scent must be lost or forgotten as the puppies grow up. Puppies which remain in the pack with the bitch always get special consideration from her and some continuing maternal attention even when they are completely adult, but those puppies which are sold are not recognised when they return to their ancestral home. They are usually treated as intruders by their mother.

Sight

In comparison with the complexity and versatility of the human eye the dog has a simple visual system. The dog cannot, for example, distinguish distant objects unless they are moving, and as far as we know, they can only see in shades of grey. A person standing against a hedge only a short distance from a dog may be invisible to it, even wearing bright clothes, if the wind is carrying the scent the other way, so it is wise to combine your commands with hand signals from the beginning to give your dog every chance to obey.

Dogs with flat faces (Boxers, Pugs, Pekes) can judge distance well but do not have long sight compared with those breeds which have one eye positioned each side of a prominent nose (Cockers, Borzois). These dogs are dependant on turning the eyes and the whole head to see what is going on all round them. It is important in this context to realise that frequent punishment by hand, rolled up newspaper or stick may make such a dog fearful of any arm movement on the edge of its vision. A dog constantly on the defensive against such a weapon may feel threatened by a lady making expansive gestures in conversation or a stranger pointing out the way over the hill.

Some of the completely unexplainable attacks made by dogs on innocent people may be due to a sudden movement of this kind at the edge of a dog's visual field, when it has been used to fearing such actions. Dominant dogs resent the threat of punishment by someone not their pack leader. Dogs tend to feel threatened by, or fear, people showing unconventional body language, such as people who are lame or have some physical disability, or those carrying unusual burdens, such as a sack over the shoulder.

Some breeds are affected by an eye disease which gradually reduces vision (Progressive Retinal Atrophy, PRA). The first sign may be a reluctance to go out at night, but if you notice that your dog is bumping into objects especially at twilight, if it cannot see to catch a ball accurately, have it examined by a veterinary surgeon at once. In some breeds, the Cairn, Corgi and Irish Setter, puppies as young as three months can be screened for PRA before there is any chance of them being used in a breeding programme. Others must wait until they are adult until they can be diagnosed as free from this degenerative but painless disease.

The eye of the dog is particularly disease-prone, different breeds having their own particular troubles. Collies and Shetland Sheepdogs have their own condition, termed Collie Eye Anomaly; Glaucoma, increased pressure within the eye which is painful, affects primarily the American Cocker Spaniel, and the Basset Hound. Lens Luxation, sudden in onset and painful, is seen mostly in the small terriers, the Tibetan Terrier, both coat types in Wire Fox Terriers, and in Jack Russells. Cataracts, an opacity of the lens, can be hereditary and in some breeds develops very soon after the puppies are born. Other malformations of the eye occur where small eyes are called for by the breed standard (the Chow Chow is an example), or where what may be termed badly designed eyes are called for, for instance the diamond-shaped eye, showing a lot of haw (the inner eyelid) in the bloodhound. In the case of any inflamatory or disease condition, or obvious failure to see, get help early from your vet, the dog's sight may be saved if you do so.

Hearing

The ear of the dog is much more acute and more discerning than our own. Dogs can hear sounds on a much higher register, so the so-called silent whistle can be used in training them.

Those breeds with pricked up, wide open ears (German Shepherd Dog, Pharaoh Hound) can suffer acutely if confined in a household where someone plays the trumpet or where the TV sound or stereo is always turned up to full strength.

Companion dogs have to cope with a deluge of sound which does not concern them and yet they can pick up a familiar word used in conversation as much as 25 yards away. Their own names are perhaps the words they are most attuned to, for they are used to hearing their name said sharply, in anger or in a caressing voice. Other words are only significant when used in the appropriate tone, as praise or admonishment.

Some very high pitched sounds seem to give dogs actual pain, and they will show fear or resentment, according to their nature, at some food mixers, or circular saws, even when they are familiar with the apparatus.

Unfamiliar noises are startling or alarming to dogs, and owners must always be aware that the dog may react badly, for instance, to children who scream while playing; to baby noises, even to people singing if it is not a normal activity in the dog's household. The noise made must be much more intense to the dog.

The location of a sound in open countryside seems difficult for dogs and they may need extra sight or scent clues to find a person calling them from a distance. Get your dog used to a combination of sign and sound commands.

Very precise identification of sounds important to the dog is possible, for instance the sound of their own food bowl is distinguished from other cooking utensils, and they soon learn to pick out the engine sound of their owner's car. It may be useful to remember that when you are moving house or decorating and rooms are empty of furniture, every sound echos in an unfamiliar way and your dog may become more care seeking for this reason.

Touch

A dog's natural response to being touched by strange hands is to recoil and be on the defensive or very submissive, according to type, but the touch of an experienced veterinary surgeon or dog handler is seldom resented, because these people approach the dog in the right way. It is foolish and dangerous to touch a strange dog of a guard breed without having permission from the owner to do so. Once accepted, touching by stroking can be a very effective rewarding action for a dog, and some smooth-coated dogs seem to receive positive comfort by being in body contact with other dogs or humans . . . they need to lie close together, and with other dogs, will pile on top of one another. It has been observed that when dogs are stimulated by sound, sight and touch at the same time, the response to touch will dominate, so it may be unproductive to try to condition a dog to react to words

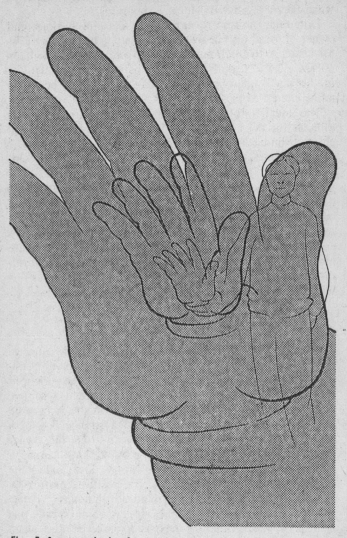

Fig. 5. A pat on the head.
   What a pat on the head looks like to a dog. See how
   threatening the human hand appears.

while touching. But we teach SIT with word and touch very successfully.

If a dog looks aggressive and dominant never try to stroke it from above, your hand may appear as a threat. Offer the back of your hand to the dog to sniff . . . on the principle that your scent will convey your good intentions, and then, if reaction is favourable, stroke the dog low down on its body.

Reflexes

As well as the need to understand its place in the pack the puppy must also learn to make the appropriate response to an outside stimulus if it is to survive. In essence, this is done by trial and error, and the dog learns by getting a pleasurable or unpleasurable reaction following a specific activity. The puppy has, by the time it is twelve weeks old already acquired a set of reflex behaviours, superimposed on inborn reflexes like sucking and feeding, urine marking and territory guarding, and maternal behaviour in the bitches. Not all dogs have inborn reflexes to the same degree; occasionally bitches lack maternal instinct, for instance.

4

HOW DOGS LEARN

LEARNING can be defined as a change in the behaviour of the animal as a result of previous experience. A learned response can be acquired from about three weeks onward by either *classical* or *instrumental* conditioning.

The well-known story of Pavlov's dogs is an example of classical conditioning. Pavlov, a Russian physiologist who died in 1936, is famous for his study of conditioned reflexes in dogs. Every time he fed his dogs he rang a bell, and after comparatively few such experiences, the dogs learnt to anticipate the arrival of food when a bell was rung, and they would salivate profusely at the sound of the bell. The sound produces a conditioned response. In the instrumental learning process the action of the dog is followed by a reward for doing some particular action. Many dogs soon learn to bark or to scratch at a door when they want to go outside or come in, and they soon learn that we will respond to their request, especially to go out, because we want them to be clean. Our very old bitch, Pooka, has learnt to exploit our reaction by barking for "out", with extreme urgency, in the middle of a TV programme or a conversation on the telephone, and then not wanting to go out at all, but having achieved her aim in gaining my attention. Dogs manipulate us too! The Doberman bitch, Anna, soon learnt that the ringing of the outside bell meant that those working outside should come into the house for a meal, so now Anna always comes to the back door when the bell rings in anticipation of a food reward.

Response to Words

Teaching dogs to respond appropriately to words said in a particular tone of voice is another example of instrumental conditioning. By trial and error the dog soon learns which response will be rewarded and those which will bring no reward.

Fight or Flight

Dogs have a very highly developed fight or flight reaction; they can muster their reactions very much quicker than most humans, the sound of something beginning to fall towards them will cause a dog to leap away from the source of danger. This is why "booby trapping" an area in which the dog is tempted to be destructive works so well, as we will describe later.

In summary, therefore, dogs learn to live with people by modifying their inherent behaviour patterns by a process of trial and error. Lessons are learnt by the receipt of rewards or punishment, and this is the method we shall exploit in teaching you to manage your dog so that it becomes a happy and fulfilled member of your family pack.

Section II

THE DOG IN YOUR HOME

5

THE DOG'S NEEDS

BEFORE you make any moves at all to choose a dog for your family, it is important to visualise what its life will be with you, not only on lovely sunny mornings but in the depths of winter when the days for exercising are very short. The place where you intend to take your dog for day-to-day exercise is an important consideration. If you have to use a public park, a very large dog or a hound type dog, prone to chase other furry creatures, may not be suitable. While large dogs do not necessarily mean to injure the small, they are inclined to show domination particularly if the small dog challenges them, as some small breeds are very inclined to do, and may hurt them unintentionally. While such a confrontation would in the vast majority of cases end amicably if the dogs were left alone, the presence of worried, perhaps screaming owners complicates and distorts the situation, and inevitably gets the larger dog a bad reputation which is often quite undeserved.

Sad though it may be to deny many worthy people the pleasure of dog ownership, we feel that it is not a good plan to acquire a dog unless you can allow it some free choice of access to the outside world; every dog needs a tiny garden, a paved patio or even a balcony to which it can come and go at will. However dutiful you may be about taking the dog out a minimum of four times a day, it seems to impose too much restriction on a dog if it can never choose for itself whether to be outside or not, can never potter about looking for the things dogs look for, free of human interference.

If you are able to allow your dog free access to a garden, then the garden must be fenced, to a height suitable to the breed. Many big dogs can jump and scramble over six feet easily and if there is any attraction in neighbouring gardens, they will do so directly your eye is off them. It is anti-social to let any dog wander off your own property besides putting your dog at risk.

It is a very good idea to get the fencing done before you get the puppy, right up to the maximum height which will be needed, rather than wait until the dog has cleared the existing fence once. Any successful action of this kind is counter-productive to keeping the dog within bounds. The dog, having been rewarded by freedom, will try again and again to jump out.

Gates should have secure fastenings, high up, but easy for all the family to use, and it is preferable if the back garden can be securely cut off from any road with motor traffic. Dogs, like children, seem attracted to get to places which afford them the greatest danger, but you cannot reason with a puppy as you could with a child.

Unsupervised dogs, particularly those which have just dashed out of an open door or gap in the hedge, have no road sense at all. They are the cause of many road accidents and their owners are liable for the damage caused to the car and the occupants.

Puppies and young dogs, or newly acquired adult dogs, do not do well where all members of the family are away for many hours of the day. Dogs get lonely and bored, and consequently noisy and destructive, and it is impossible to teach a puppy good behaviour unless there is someone present to correct it when it does wrong, or praise it when it does well. When dogs are alerted by a caller at the house, many will continue to bark for hours unless checked and there will be, quite justly, complaints by the neighbours. A mature dog may be left safely for four to five hours sometimes but even this should not be on a regular basis.

As a dog breeder I am often asked to let a puppy go to someone who works "mornings only". I find this situation unacceptable since in the very nature of things the dog will not be exercised enough to be tired before the family leaves for work in the morning. All the alerting noises of tradesmen happen in the morning too, and a working session of four hours can often mean a six-hour stretch away from home by the time the shopping is done as well. "Afternoons only" is a better proposition, but neither is ideal.

More and more employers allow well behaved dogs to accompany staff to work (the guard dog element can be a persuasive factor) and it may be possible to allow the dog to remain in your car part of the day, but remember how easily a stationary car heats up in summer and be sure to park in the shade and allow plenty of ventilation.

Your working day will inevitably be broken up by the need to attend to the dog, but this is only one example of the "sacrifices" you will have to make if you take a dog into your family as a dependent to be cared for and planned for.

You may feel that taking on an older dog may be easier, but dogs looking for second or third owners usually have some behaviour or personality fault which has caused them to be unwanted by the original owners. You may not find out the snags until a crisis occurs. Alternatively, you may be lucky in being able to take on a well-loved pet which the previous owners cannot keep for some viable reason. In taking on an adult dog it is all the more necessary not to leave it alone for any length of time until you thoroughly understand the way it reacts and until the dog feels really secure in your home. Newly acquired adult dogs are very easily lost when off the lead, either because they become disorientated, do not recognise you as their owner, or because they are attempting to return to their first home. Even if the dog is good at "come when called" in the garden, do not rely on your control over it outside the home until two or three months have passed.

6

CHOOSING A DOG

DOGS which have been in rescue homes for many weeks may have been "conditioned" to become jumpers, wire biters, barkers and general escapologists just by prolonged confinement in kennels. It may be the case that they are only there because they are incorrigible wanderers or the canine equivalent of sex maniacs. Sad as it is to say, the odds against making a successful pet out of the flotsam of the canine world are very great.

The older dog which is surplus to requirements at a breeding or showing kennel also has disadvanatges; it may never have lived in a house, may not be vert attuned to people but much more dependent on canine company. Busy kennels feed, walk and groom dogs in the course of the day's work but the opportunity for human-to-dog communication is relatively small; the kennelised dog may have difficulty in adapting to the more variable life of a household. Kennel life normally allows dogs access to a small outside run for all the daylight hours and such dogs may resent being shut in a house. They are used to being able to excrete day or night wherever they wish within their territory, so you will have a lot of pre-formed habit to break down in that area.

The kennel dog has often had its natural intelligence damped down by under-use, and it may be difficult to awake much response to further teaching, or there may be a whole world of affection and cleverness just waiting to be released by individual attention from an owner. There an be no doubt that the well-reared, well-conditioned puppy is the best material for a successful family pet.

The basic decision is between Pedigreed, Cross-bred or Mongrel. Mongrel litters are seldom deliberately bred, they are nature's accidents and so it follows that the litter is unlikely to have had as much care, conditioning and know-ledge behind it as the pedigree litter.

The product of several generations of wanderers as most mongrel litters are, is unlikely to be easy to keep at home, and you will not know what "ingredients" you have in your puppy. Knowing the in-bred character traits is a great help in managing your puppy.

Crossbreds, that is the product of two known, pedigreed dogs, are sometimes known as "Kennel Maid's accidents". The inadvertent pairing of dog and bitch does happen in the best run kennels and the result may be an unorthodox but well-reared puppy, provided the nature of the two parents are compatible. Pairings between varieties of gun-dog, or Collie cross gundogs seem to work well. In mongrel and cross-bred matings the puppies are often larger than the parents, and the coat tends to be smooth more often than rough, and seldom silky. It is also interesting that where short faces are paired with long, the short face is entirely lost in the first generation and not regained . . . you never see a pug-faced mongrel, and Boxer crosses are always long nosed but tend to have Boxer body shape.

Your reception will not be cordial if you telephone your local kennel asking if they have any "accidents" to dispose of . . . they are likely to deny that any such thing could ever happen. You get to hear of these puppies by word of mouth or by advertisements in the local press. Do not buy a *cross-bred* unless you see the puppies with their mother; you must be sure of at least half of the partnership and preferably both halves.

There are more than 140 separate breeds of pedigreed dogs, so there is bound to be one which suits your lifestyle and your inclination, but as with marriage, you will be unwise to choose entirely by looks. The dog you are buying should be part of your family for about ten years at least, and you will have in that time to spend a lot of money and a lot of care and affection upon it, so it makes sense to take plenty of time and trouble to choose your dog, and never to buy on impulse.

Many families are stampeded into buying a puppy because they have promised the children to get one and

once the intention is declared, the children will not wait.
The best advice is to keep your intentions secret while you
do the preliminary exploration and even the final choosing;
this is an area where adults should have the final word.
There is nothing more embarrassing than to have to drag
children away from a kennel as they wail "Why won't you
buy a puppy from that lady, Daddeeee . . ."

Hair Shedding

All dogs have to get rid of their dead hair coat in some
way . . . most shed hair, but the Poodle and Bedlington
have theirs cut off, rather expensively, at six-weekly
intervals. These last two breeds may be suitable, however,
for asthmatic patients allergic to ordinary dog hair. Dogs
used to be said to moult twice a year, but since we have
taken many heavy-coated dogs to live in our centrally
heated houses, they lose hair all the year round. Surprisingly, really long hair can be easier to remove from
carpets than the hair from short-coated dogs which can
become imbedded in fabric.

If you buy a long-haired dog, grooming must be done
every day, in order to keep the underlying skin healthy and
to keep the dog acceptable in your home . . . a matted
coat is a degradation to the dog and renders it unsuitable
to be in the house. One factor to consider is where the
grooming is to be done, you will not want to brush the dog
and have the debris flying about your living quarters. Dogs
with corded coats, the Puli and the Komondor, can take
the place of handicraft work for their owners, you can
twirl the hair into cords while watching television!

Dogs with soft woolly undercoats (German Shepherds,
Corgis), can be a real problem at some times of the year
when the coat comes out in handfuls. It is best to take the
dog into the garden and strip out as much as possible.

The next choice lies between large, medium or small
dog, a weight range between about 4 lbs (1.8 kg), in the
Chihuahua, and 140–150 lbs (63–68kg), in the Newfound-
land and something for all tastes in between.

Large dogs fill a very different role in the family than
that of the tiny pet, which is essentially a cuddle-object,

a comforter, an amusement, or a little status symbol. There is always an ego-boost for the person who can "do what they like" with a dog which weighs as much or more than many humans; the affection of such a powerful creature does confer a special blessing. Big dogs have shoulders to cry on and sides you can slap, and even those not specially bred for guard tendencies look forbidding enough to the prospective intruder. Not all large dogs are greedy for exercise, some, like the Mastiff, are quite lethargic; some, like the Wolfhound, will curl down into quite a small space, but others, notably the Setters and Dalmatians, must have rooms big enough for them to turn around without swishing all the things off the coffee table with their tails. You can get a St Bernard into a tiny car, but it feels uncomfortable and looks rather silly, and big dogs do like to retain their dignity.

In describing so many breeds in a few words it is inevitable that some injustice will be done by too much generalisation, but it is as well to be aware of the characteristics of some of the most popular breeds because this should influence your choice quite profoundly. Remember that large dogs will need the most expensive size in collars, beds, and feeding bowls; that their veterinary bills will in most cases be larger, as larger doses of drugs are used, and they require larger accommodation at boarding kennels, and eat more.

On the other hand, there are expenses which do not vary with breed; preventative vaccinations cost the same for the tiny or the largest dog; premiums for third party insurance and to cover veterinary treatment are the same, and a railway ticket for a dog accompanying a passenger is charged at identical rate for a Beagle or a Saint Bernard.

The smallest dogs can be too fragile for family life, very fine bones are easily broken and joints may be displaced in a well-meant rough and tumble. Papillons, Chihuahuas, Yorkies and Toy Poodles suit adult homes best, and are ideal for those who must travel by public transport, as they are easy to carry on buses, and will travel free on trains provided they are in a container carried by the passenger.

It is important to remember that dogs glorified by

exposure on advertisements, in cartoons and in television appearances are not necessarily, or even likely to be as accommodating and adaptable as they seem. The Old English Sheepdog and the Basset Hound are two breeds that come to mind as having been exploited shamefully in this way and a great many families have been very disappointed when they got these dogs into their homes. We watch the Border Collies at Sheepdog trials with great admiration, but these dogs are under strong domination by the handlers, and they are given long days at work which curbs their energy. In idleness, the Border Collie can become hysterical, and a *sheep chaser*. This breed is quick to learn but it must do something with the skill it acquires, either the work for which it was bred, or else have the mental stimulus of competing in Obedience Trials.

The Hound breeds are conditioned to hunt, by sight or by scent, and the compulsion to do so can make them take every opportunity to escape from house and garden, or from control when on a walk. Afghans and Salukis, hounds which hunt by sight, can almost never be let off the lead in open country, as even their greatest devotees have to admit that these hounds seldom obey a command when running free. Basenjis are mischievous, may climb on top of your highest cupboard, but they are fun to own. While not having the bark of other dogs, they do have a yodel, and are by no means silent. Dachshunds were taught to bark while they were underground, flushing fox and badger out of their lairs. This breed still has the persistent loud bark and they are also great diggers, so you will have to bury your boundary fence deep into the ground. Beagles are the ideal size and shape for companion dogs and they have lovely temperament but they will escape if they get the chance.

Best companion material among the hounds: Finnish Spitz and Whippets. Absolutely unsuitable for novice owners: ex-pack Foxhounds, Otterhounds, Bloodhounds, Borzois, and Afghans and Salukis unless you have several acres of fenced ground available.

Gundogs usually have good temperament and mix happily with other dogs, but they are capable of working all day in bad weather, and confinement is therefore frustrating and can cause a deterioration in temperament. Golden Retrievers and Labradors are among the kindest dogs known. They make splendid companions for children as they will retrieve and play hide and seek endlessly. Both these breeds are used extensively as Guide Dogs for the Blind, a tribute to their ability to take direction and training, but they must have mental and physical activity every day. All the Setters are lively, high-spirited dogs, they remain puppyish for a long time.

The Weimaraner's unique silver-grey colouring makes it very attractive, but temperament is not as easy as in other gundogs, and they need work.

The Cocker Spaniel is now rarely used as a gundog and over-popularity immediately post-World War II contributed to a deterioration in temperament in the black and the red colouring. The coats of the blacks need regular trimming. English and Welsh Springer Spaniels have good temperament which can be spoilt by a too restrictive life. The untrained gundog is always liable to take off after game on a country walk often with disastrous results.

Best Companion Dog material: The Labrador, Golden Retriever and the Pointer.

Terriers were bred to hunt rodents; their special attributes are keenness, persistence and quick snapping jaws. Temperaments are good, not too dependent on owner company and with the ability to keep busy on their own in the garden. The snatching habit of the terriers may make them unsuitable where there are toddler-age children in the family.

Most terriers need professional stripping, by terrier specialists, twice a year to keep them in good shape, the Border Terrier is an exception.

Bull Terriers and Staffordshire Bull Terriers are the result of 18th and 19th century crosses to provide keen determined dogs for bull baiting and fighting. Both breeds still enjoy a good scrap but are wonderfully devoted family pets and are trustworthy with children. They are not quite so dependent on human company as the proper Bull breeds, having a modification of terrier self-reliance.

Good Companion Dog Material: Border Terrier, Cairn Terrier, Staffordshire Bull Terrier.

Shepherding Dogs: The German Shepherd Dog (Alsatian), is the world's most popular dog and rightly so. The many different duties it performs as Guide Dog, and with the police and the armed forces of the world are a tribute to this dog's versatility, but they may be shy and therefore untrustworthy. It has a very strong guarding instinct which is easily misdirected and this dog must have sensible, but never harsh handling. It is essential to take veterinary advice before buying a German Shepherd because they can have a number of hereditary problems. The Briard is a French herding dog, shaggy coated, very good natured and rapidly becoming popular. Of the Collies, the Bearded Collie is the most suitable family dog; Shetland Sheepdogs can be shy and have a high-pitched bark; Rough Collies (Lassie-dogs), may resent visitors to the family. The Border Collie excels at Obedience work. Many people will have admired their ability in sheep herding competitions but may have failed to observe that the dogs are under very strong dominance by their handlers. These dogs, taken so recently from a working background, must have something to do in their day. All sheep herding dogs may, if untrained, become *sheep chasers.*

Best companion dog material: Bearded Collie, Briard.

Not for novices: The Old English Sheepdog (because of grooming problems).

The Guarding Breeds: These are power-packed dogs, capable of inflicting serious injury on an intruder or anyone making an attack upon their owner, but they are very agreeable and tolerant within the family. Because a guard dog may sometimes misinterpret a caller's intention, all guarding breeds must be kept under strict supervision and they must respond to command instantly. Most guarding breeds tend to want to dominate other dogs, so they are not suitable to exercise off the lead in public parks. The European man-made breeds of the 19th century figure prominently among the modern guard dogs, the Doberman, Boxer, Rottweiler and Giant Schnauzer are examples.

Boxers are the most exuberant and boisterous of the guarding breeds; they are great playmates for older children and well liked by publicans and hotel keepers . . . the Boxer loves people as long as people are doing the right things. Bred, like the Rottweiler, to be a personal guard and companion, these dogs expect to be with people constantly and they are very poor "yard guards", doing their best work from an armchair in the hall. Dobermans are more elegant to look at, but sharper in their work, being used by some police forces. Bull Mastiffs are placid, Mastiffs even more so, except when guarding ability is needed.

When looking at the pedigrees of any of these breeds and the German Shepherd, with a view to buying a companion dog with guarding ability, it would be wise to avoid litters with imported German dogs close up in the pedigree. Dogs of the guarding breeds in Germany must pass an "ability to attack" test before they can be used for breeding, and the temperament is therefore sharper than we like in this country.

None of these dogs need training to guard, the instinct is there and will come to the surface when needed however soft your dog may appear in daily life. It is extremely dangerous to encourage any of these breeds to show aggression, even as a joke.

Best companion dog material for family wanting guarding dog: Boxer for laughs, Doberman for serious deterrent.

The Bernese Mountain Dog, adept at pulling carts, makes a genial but large companion for children. Welsh Corgis were bred to herd and drive cattle by nipping the heels of the laggards. Essentially a working farm dog, they were not kept as pets until taken up by the Royal family in the 1930s. Corgis still have to be shown from a very early age that biting is against the rules.

Bulldogs are slow movers, obstinate, not very long lived, but cheerful and good tempered. As they walk at a slow amble, they are very well suited to adults with the same inclinations. French Bulldogs are smaller, lively and affectionate and like the Boston Terrier, have a lot of the bull-

breed attributes in a small package, they are highly recom-
mended.

The Tibetan dogs, Shih Tzu, Tibetan Terrier, Lhasa
Apsos and Tibetan Spaniel have shrill penetrating voices,
they were alleged to bark a warning of approaching travellers from the ramparts of the monasteries. The first three
Tibetan breeds require a lot of grooming. Schipperkes and
Keeshonds are also "warning" dogs but not guards, very
agreeable as pets.

Poodles are among the most versatile of all companion
dogs, much more down to earth than their show appearance would indicate.

Among the toy dogs there are miniature versions of
many of the large breeds. The Cavalier King Charles
Spaniel is the largest of the breeds termed "Toy". They
have some of the hunting attributes of the spaniel but most
of the breed are submissive in character, unassuming with
other dogs and easy to board as they settle with anyone
who is kind to them. Some owners may find the modern
Cavalier a little lacking in character. The Yorkshire Terrier
is still a superb ratter when not hampered by excess coat.
Pugs and Pekes need to keep their cool, both in fights with
other dogs and in the conditions in which they live. Their
breathing apparatus is soon overtaxed in warm weather
and stuffy rooms.

Chihuahuas are not very friendly to visitors and are not
children's dogs.

Best companion dog material in small package: Look
at the Tibetan Spaniel (Peke-like but more athletic), the
sporty Griffon, and the larger Poodles and poodle cross
terriers. Many apologies to all the breeds there was not
room to mention.

Some of the most popular breeds which make good
companion dog material have some inherited physical
defects, only seen as the dog gets older. Breeders are in
the main working very hard to eliminate disease from their
stock, but it is essential to get veterinary advice before you
buy German Shepherd Dog, Miniature and Toy Poodle,
Labrador, Golden Retriever and Cocker Spaniel.

Puppies should be bought direct from a breeder, where

you can see the mother with her litter, and possibly some other related dogs as well. If choosing a large breed, it is a great advantage to see some adolescent dogs, rough and boisterous, and not to make your decision only on the basis of the quiet maternal bitch and little puppies. Your own summing up of the breeder's attitude, the surroundings in which the puppies are being reared, and the advice and friendship of the breeder who takes continuing interest in the puppies after sale is of inestimable benefit to you. None of these advantages will be yours if you buy from a pet shop, or a dealer where puppies are bought in from a variety of sources. Veterinary surgeons have declared that it is a handicap affecting physical and mental health for a puppy to move homes more than once before twelve weeks of age.

All dogs are expensive to rear well; you pay not only for the puppy but for all the care given to the mother before the birth and the fee paid for the use of the stud dog.

Exotic and rare breeds newly imported to this country obviously cost more and those where the bitches have trouble giving birth, for instance, Bulldogs, are always expensive; breeds which have large litters, Irish Setters, Labradors, come much cheaper than tiny Yorkshire Terriers, that breed is almost international currency these days.

The Purchase

It makes sense to buy your puppy as close to your home as possible. You will have all the benefit of keeping in touch with the breeder and the puppy will have only a short journey to your home. Your local veterinary surgeon may be able to advise you about litters which are due; in any case, it is wise to contact a veterinary practice before you make the purchase. Most veterinary surgeons will advise prospective owners about the suitability of the breed it is proposed to get, and this service is usually free of charge. If you want the vet to actually examine the puppy for fitness, this will command a fee but it will be money well spent. If there should be anything drastically wrong with the puppy you have chosen, it is much better to know at once, before you have got so fond of the little dog that you feel obliged to keep it. You could let yourself in for a trying time, both financially and emotionally, if you take on an ailing puppy.

Your vet may not know of a breeder in the immediate vicinity but having contacted a veterinary practice, there is a network of knowledge open to you. The nurses and the receptionists are likely to be interested in dogs, they may take the two weekly dog newspapers, *Dog World* and *Our Dogs*, which contain many advertisements by breeders. You will also find puppies advertised in local papers (approach with care and make enquiries before committing yourself), or the Kennel Club will let you have a list of breeders in your area; write to 1 Clarges Street, London, W.1.

Responsible breeders do not have puppies available all the time. Many of the people who supply the best companion stock breed only occasionally, when they have compiled a waiting list for puppies. More and more breeders are feeling that it is unethical to have litters of puppies available to sell to impulse buyers, so when you do locate a litter you may find they are all booked. Disappointing though this may be at the time, it augurs well for the puppy that you will buy from such a breeder in the future, for a puppy programmed to be a companion dog from the start is what you are looking for. As litters do not always provide the sexes in the ratio required, you may find some puppies unbooked, but then your choice is limited.

It is difficult to get puppy buyers to look beyond the skin, and buyers frequently ask for a "red dog with one white sock just like our old Kim" . . . but surely it was character that made Kim so beloved and not really his overcoat? The pick of the litter is usually taken to mean the puppy with all features corresponding as far as is possible in one so young, with the Kennel Club standard for the breed.

Choosing a companion by evaluation of temperament allows you to consider the whole litter, including mismarked puppies.

It is important, before making any more progress with your plans, to be sure that everyone in the family and even those people who work in your house and garden really want a puppy and will follow out your plan for management. Just one person who feels aggravated or resentful can ruin your scheme and one person over-indulgent or too sympathetic can do just as much harm. People play out a lot of their own resentments and spites via the family dog, and this is especially true where the new puppy causes some employee more work or trouble.

The characters of two bitches were very much influenced by a gardener employed when they were young, although he only saw them for a few hours in the week. We found out that he used to kick at them when they were mischievous. One of the bitches has a long-term grudge against anyone in wellington boots or pushing a barrow, while the other is timid and has to be encouraged to remain on her feet when unfamiliar men are around. Quite a small amount of unkind or unjust treatment seems to outweigh the understanding these dogs normally received.

A point for very close consideration is the attitude of the women of the family, are they being honest and truthful about their wish to have a dog? As a generalisation, women like to please their men and children, and will loyally declare that they do indeed long for a dog about the place. Unfortunately, some dogs are unsuccessful pets because the women in the home had not pictured just how much more housework the dog would make, or how much the new puppy would curb their freedom. Care of the dog so often devolves on the one at home all day and a desire to please the rest of the family cannot always be maintained when coping with the actuality of the dog underfoot.

In order to manage the puppy skilfully, it must be *wanted* by *all* the family, and they must *all* feel equal good-will towards it. The dog that is shut out all day in order to save pawmarks on the kitchen floor, or the dog that is unreasonably chastised when it cannot associate punishment with the deed may grow into a nervous animal, and only then will you realise that someone has not been following the family's plan for its management.

The confident, happy dog, which feels that the world is a reliable place where human behaviour is consistent, is the dog which will bring you compliments everywhere.

Sometimes parents are motivated to get a dog because one of their children has developed an unreasonable fear of dogs. It is better to break down the phobia by periodic association with a reliable, co-operative older dog before you introduce a dog or puppy into your own household. A dog may be adversely affected by a show of fear; it would be reasonable to expect a puppy to run after a child which runs away from it, but if the child is running in fear, the puppy will have to be restrained. A dominant puppy in such a situation may perceive the child to be subordinate in ranking, and the child may then have genuine reason to be afraid of the dog. Normality in approach by everyone concerned must be the keynote in managing your puppy correctly.

Check List of Considerations for Dog Ownership

1. Have we sufficient space for a dog indoors and out?

2. Can we provide companionship and interest for the dog for the greater part of each day, especially when it is young?

3. Is our garden sufficiently well fenced to keep a dog in?

4. Where will we take the dog for exercise, away from motor traffic and where it can be let off the lead easily and regularly?

5. Can we afford to feed a dog properly and pay for regular vaccinations and boosters to protect it from disease?

6. Have we budgeted for veterinary fees in illness and accident or for an insurance policy to cover those fees and our third party liability if our dog should cause an injury or damage another person's property?

7. Is our family or our environment likely to change in the foreseeable future, making the conditions for having a dog less suitable?

8. Can we make plans for the dog when we go on holiday, have we budgeted for boarding kennel expenses?

9. Do all the family really want a dog and are we willing to be responsible owners, not allowing our dog to be a nuisance in any way?

10. Are we happy to accept the inconveniences associated with dog ownership?

11. Have we the time to look after a dog, now and in the foreseeable future?

Check List for Choice of Dog

1. Do we want a pedigreed dog or a mongrel?
2. Do we prefer small, medium or large dogs?
3. Is that size the most suitable for our home, car and exercise ground?
4. Do we want a sporting dog, a guard, a ratter, runner or a cuddle object?
5. Do we like smooth or hairy coats, silky or rough?
6. Is anyone in the family allergic to dog hair?
7. Do we understand the grooming requirements of the dog we are considering, will we actually groom it often enough, have we somewhere to do the grooming, in summer and winter?
8. Do we want a puppy or an adult dog?
9. Do we want a dog or a bitch or does it not matter?
10. Can we cope with a pushy, dominant dog or will a submissive one be more suitable? Or one in between?

7

DOG OR BITCH?

THE next big decision is whether to have a dog or a bitch in the breeds that attract you. In some of the smaller, submissive breeds there is very little character difference between the two sexes, but in breeds where all the individuals tend to be to some degree dominant, the difference in behaviour between male and female is usually more marked. Males tend to be more self-reliant, harder characters, possibly even defiant at times in adolescence, and males may also develop embarrassing behaviour traits, but this book should be able to help you there.

The bitches are, on the whole, more affectionate and biddable. Where dogs tend to proclaim their dominance over unfamiliar canines, bitches are less inclined to do so outside the home, so in "fighting" breeds the bitch is a better choice for exercising in public places. There are, of course, bitches with masculine tendencies and dogs that are softer characters.

Where a large breed animal is to be with women and children for most of the day a bitch is preferable and will have no less a guarding ability than the male. If there is one dog already in the household or one which is a regular visitor, it makes sense to have a new pet of the same sex. The complications of dog/bitch encounters (unless one is neutered), are too great for the average household, and it is verging on cruelty to attempt to keep a dog in the same house as an in-season bitch.

The Bitch

All bitches are subject to some degree of hormonally controlled mood swing from the time they reach puberty. This should occur between the age of 8–12 months and thereafter heat will occur at 6–10 month intervals for the rest of her life, unless some measures are taken to avert the breeding cycle. There is no menopause in the bitch.

The average bitch will show some heightened excitability in her behaviour for a week or two before her season begins. You may also notice that the bitch does some urine marking to spread the news of her forthcoming

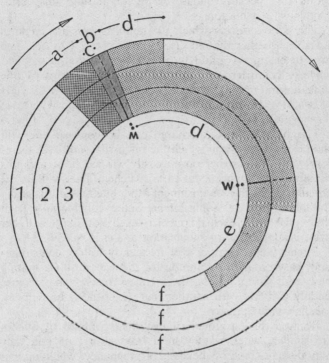

Fig. 6. Band 1 **normal cycle**. a. Attractiveness to males. b. Acceptance of male. c. Spontaneous ovulation. d. Sexual activity wanes 15 days. a – d. Heat. f. Sexual inactivity 5 – 7 months.
Band 2. Normal cycle with false pregnancy. a – c as above. d. 63 days build up to false pregnancy. w. Imaginary whelping and nursing and/or actual lactation. f. Sexual inactivity $4\frac{1}{2}$ – $5\frac{1}{2}$ mths.
Band 3. Normal cycle with pregnancy. a – c as above. m. Mating. d. 63 days pregnancy. e. Actual lactation and nursing. f. Sexual inactivity $3\frac{1}{2}$ – $5\frac{1}{2}$ months.

season. Once the heat starts, her vulva begins to swell and changes go on in the vagina which will result in the blood-stained discharge which is characteristic of the start of heat. The vulval discharge of a bitch on heat lasts for about 18 days, changing from blood to straw coloured in that time. The tenth day of heat is the time when the bitch shows an especially intense desire for mating; this corresponds with ovulation.

The period during which the bitch accepts the male is variable, whether the red discharge has ceased or not. The urge to be mated gradually wanes, the discharge pales to white or colourless and then ceases, and the vulva returns to its normal size at between 21 and 28 days from the start of heat. At this time it is safe to allow the bitch with male dogs again.

The blood-stained discharge can be copious and will stain every surface on which the bitch sits. You will therefore want to keep her on an easily washed floor and this usually means banishment to the kitchen. This will almost certainly seem like "punishment" to a bitch used to sharing the family fireside. Some bitches suffer considerably from this undeserved exclusion which need not happen if her cycle is suppressed by medication or she is spayed.

Bitches kept together will frequently follow each other into season and it is common for them to simulate mating play and mounting together. Unless one bitch becomes unduly irritable with another there is no need to suppress this behaviour pattern.

Because the hormonal changes in the blood of bitches are similar, whether they have been mated or not, they may display some of the signs of pregnancy, whelping and lactation during the six to eight weeks following the start of heat. This condition is called false pregnancy. At its greatest intensity, an unmated bitch can show a bodily enlargement which mimics pregnancy, she may make a nest, produce milk and attempt to mother inanimate objects or her own toys with all the devotion she would extend to a live litter. A strongly-affected bitch, guarding a litter which is visible only to her can be a danger when children approach her although her normal temperament may be excellent. The bitch with a false pregnancy and litter is more emotionally disturbed than one which has actual puppies to guard.

Even a mild false pregnancy can make the bitch feel off-colour and inclined to mope and, unfortunately, when it has happened once, the false pregnancy and nursing behaviour is likely to occur after every heat and the tendency is not alleviated by letting the bitch have an actual litter, it may even make her more intense next time.

The remedy is to have the bitch spayed (a surgical operation to remove the uterus and ovaries so that she will not experience a hormonal cycle), or to employ some form of contraception, in pill form or by injection. The latter methods are now very successful in the bitch and will save all the trauma of season and false pregnancies whilst leaving open the possibilities of breeding at some stage in her life. Bitches that are kept out of season by these modern contraceptive methods are more consistently companionable and are less likely to suffer from disease of the uterus or mammary tumours. You are strongly advised to discuss this aspect of bitch ownership with your veterinary surgeon when or before you buy your bitch puppy or, at any rate, just before or immediately after her first season. If you already have an adult bitch, the best time to consult is about one month before her next season is due.

8

BUYING YOUR PUPPY

THE final consideration in your selection process should be to look to the future. While the young men in the family may urge you towards a bouncy, active dog, will they be going away to work or University, leaving the dog to bounce on older people? A young married couple may enjoy taking a Setter or Pointer long-distance walking, but when children are born, it can be extraordinarily irksome to give the dog the vigorous exercise it requires when prams and pushchairs slow up progress, and the wife at home cannot leave the children to take the dog for a good walk.

If there is the possibility of having to take an elderly or infirm person to live in the household, the dog chosen must be large enough not to be tripped over and of steady temperament so that it does not make sudden movements . . . a Bulldog would be ideal.

Try to see the breeds you are considering in the homes of friends that own them. Stop owners in the street and ask about their dogs, where they got them, what they are like to live with, and the address of their vet. You are now an intending member of the dog owner's club and you will find that all the members delight in talking about their animals and can be a great deal of help to you. You can also see many breeds at dog shows but remember the behaviour and demeanour there may be very different to the same breed at home as a companion.

The time at which you buy your puppy is also crucial to its future good management; the puppy should come into your home when you have few outside engagements, and are not expecting visitors. Christmas and other festivals are generally most inappropriate times to introduce a new puppy. Your aim should be to concentrate nearly all your attention on the puppy for the first few weeks you have it . . . the more time you can devote during this period to seeing that it does the right things rather than the wrong ones, the more successful its upbringing will be.

It will entirely upset the puppy's training if it has to go into boarding kennels for more than a day or two before it is six months old, so if there is a holiday on the horizon, you will have to make plans for the puppy too.

New dog owners may be glad to be reminded that dogs, cats and other small pets cannot be brought into the British mainland (except from Eire and the Channel Islands and other off-shore islands), unless prior arrangements have been made for them to go into a quarantine kennel for the statutory period, currently six months. Great Britain is one of the few countries of the world free of rabies and all animal owners will want to keep it that way.

Smuggling a pet in from abroad is not only against the law, it is a wicked act against fellow dog owners and anyone who suspects that you have a dog with you illegally is likely to inform against you, for this is one evasion of Customs and Excise scrutiny that no-one will find clever or funny. The penalties for illegal entry of animals are heavy, involving prison, fines of up to £1,000 and possibly destruction of the animal concerned. The barrier on re-entry to Britain applies to the animal you took on a sail across the channel on your boat, or the one which left Britain with you in your caravan for a fortnight's holiday in Europe, as well as the deprived creature you found or bought while you were away.

KEEP RABIES OUT OF BRITAIN

Final Warnings
1. Never buy a dog on impulse, or for emotional reasons.
2. Never buy a dog as a surprise present.
3. Never buy an undersized or ailing dog because you are sorry for it.
4. Never buy a breed of dog without talking to other owners and if possible seeing some of the dogs in ordinary homes as well as in a breeder's kennels, or at a show.

If you are "on the waiting list" of a breeder, it should be possible for you to have a preliminary look at the litter at about four weeks old. The arrival of a new and highly infectious disease, Canine Parvovirus, has made breeders rather wary of infection being brought to their puppy quarters, as this virus is easily carried on human clothing and shoes. You may be asked to undergo some disinfection routine.

Seeing the litter from which you hope to make your choice is a very exciting moment. It will be useful to have seen the bitch before and during her pregnancy, as she will be not quite her normal self when worried about visitors to her litter, so you should have satisfied yourself that her temperament is good. You will have already decided whether your family group is best suited by an outgoing "pushy" puppy or a quieter one. Do please resist the impulse to abandon all the research you have done so far by snatching up the poor little puppy which looks as if it most needs the advantages you have to offer. "Poor little puppies", even at reduced price, are very poor bargains indeed and the breeder should not offer them to clients.

Fig. 7. **Puppy dominance.**
Or possibly precocious sexual behaviour.

You should also be wary of choosing an orphan or singleton puppy, as, reared alone it has a more than average chance of being maladjusted, and is a particularly unwise choice if you should want to breed later as it may lack maternal instinct.

At a few weeks old, puppies vary in their ability according to breed, the small breeds being slower to develop. Even large breed puppies play for only a short time and sleep a great deal and this sleep is very necessary for correct development of sound temperament. It is understandable that the breeder will be unwilling to wake puppies so that you may see them play.

It is an advantage to have ample time to sit and watch the puppies, but for a lengthy stay you will need to keep the party small, including only those adults vitally concerned and leaving, the children elsewhere. It cannot be too much emphasised that this is a very important buying expedition for you and it would be a pity to make the wrong choice, after so much preliminary thought, just because a crowd of people distracted you. Many people think that "going to see some puppies" is a pleasant expedition on which it would be appropriate to take neighbours, relatives and friends and their children too. Would you take them when you go to buy a new car or a washing machine? The puppy is a much more important buy, warranting a lot of discussion and thought. You may feel a bit mean excluding the children, but baby puppies do not fascinate children for long . . . five minutes and they are clamouring to be away to see some more. It is not really fair on the breeder who has so much to tell you, to complicate the conversation by bringing a large party.

Many people feel slightly embarrassed to visit a litter in the breeder's home. They think that the more impersonal atmosphere of a pet shop or a puppy dealer might be easier for them. In fact, the ethical breeder *is much more anxious* than the other outlets to place the puppies in permanent homes where they are suitable for the family concerned, and as explained earlier, there are many practical advantages in buying from a breeder. It may be, that after discussion the breeder may feel obliged to say that the puppies on offer will not suit you . . . this would be a rare reaction in a more commercial business! This advice may not at the time seem acceptable to you but please try to take it in good part. You are not being insulted, rather look upon the good side, the breeder knows the dogs better than you, and you are more than likely being saved from making an expensive and perhaps heart-rending mistake.

This first visit to the litter should be used, on your part, to assess the general health of the litter and the surroundings in which it is being reared. If you are satisfied, you should at this stage make a tentative reservation, but you must count on making another visit when the puppies are between five and six weeks old to make your final choice. At that time, if you choose one, you should expect to deposit a substantial part of the purchase price, the balance to be paid at the time of collection. If you make a tentative reservation and then think better of it, do please let the breeder know, so that the puppy can be offered again. If you regress on the bargain after a deposit has been paid, you may have to forfeit part of that deposit to pay the expenses of advertising and keeping the puppy until another buyer is found.

If you are buying a pedigreed dog you are entitled to expect that the litter will have been recorded at the Kennel Club so that if you should wish to show the dog, or breed later on, there will be no barrier to doing so. You may well find the puppies have all been individually registered with the breeder's Kennel Club prefix and in this case you will later be given a "transfer form" (make sure that the breeder has signed it), so that the dog can be recorded as in your ownership at the Kennel Club.

You should also receive a signed copy of the pedigree, and it is as well to understand the value of this piece of paper. At present there is no positive identification of dogs in Great Britain, so it is a matter of trust between breeder/Kennel Club and purchaser that the particulars on the pedigree form refer to the puppy you are buying. The pedigree is merely a record of the dog's ancestry going back four or five generations. Those much quoted "pedigrees as long as your arm" are really only so much spoiled paper, because dogs beyond the fourth generation have really very little influence on the puppy in your arms. If you do not know what those dogs looked like and how they behaved, the pedigree does not tell you much.

If there are champions (usually written in red), among the parents and grandparents of your puppy, you can conclude that these dogs looked typical of their kind but you cannot tell anything about their behaviour. If the breeder has had this line of dogs for several generations, breeding from daughters and grand-daughters of the original stock, you can go some way in concluding that line has been satisfactory in temperament, but not all the way. As we have said, keen exhibitors sometimes keep dogs for other reasons than good temperament and learning ability. While beauty shows are demanding of dogs in some ways, requiring the ability to travel very long distances and to wait for hours often in conditions of discomfort, the show dog does not need to be as versatile, adaptable and intelligent as the family pet.

The following pages of tests for puppy temperament are not conclusive, but may prove a useful guide to the way each puppy will face the experiences of the future. The scoring should be interpreted with due regard to the breed concerned; for instance, a frightened Cavalier, a breed well known to be "babyish", is not such a failure as a Doberman puppy in the same test, as this breed should be fearless. The handling test is also influenced by the amount of handling the puppies have been used to, and the skill and confidence of the unfamiliar handler. Human babies react badly to people that hold them awkwardly.

Puppies should be tested, if possible, in an unfamiliar room, one at a time. Testing should be done on a day when they have not been vaccinated and are not being wormed, and when they are about five weeks old.

Choose a well-adjusted puppy, one that is average in reaction, not the one which hangs back all the time, but one that is bright and alert, and comes to investigate what is happening when you clap your hands or lean over the play pen. A well-adjusted puppy should let you pick it up and handle it without crying; hold the puppy up and stare at it, hold it down and then turn it on its back, the puppy which will make good companion dog material should endure all these things without too much protest, certainly without being either fierce or panicked. If you make your choice after testing in this way, it is much more likely that your puppy will be resilient to all the experiences which will come its way.

Having made your final choice, it makes sound sense to arrange for a veterinary surgeon to check the prospective purchase for congenital problems like umbilical hernia, faulty knee joints, or skin conditions which could involve

Puppy Called Towards Tester

Eager Approach score (4), Approach with
Suspicion (3), Hesitant Approach (2), Unwilling
to Approach (1).   Score ☐

Free Running Behaviour

Follows Feet Eagerly score (4), Follows Feet Biting
Ankles (3), Hesitant to Follow (2), Refuses or
Runs Away (1).   Score ☐

Reaction to Sudden Noise

Interest score (2), Fear (1).   Score ☐

Reaction to Unfamiliar Moving Object

Attack score (3), Interest (2), Fear (1).   Score ☐

Reaction to Restraint by Human

Struggles Fiercely and Bites score (4), Struggles
Then Settles Down (3), Enjoys Handling (2),
Frightened (1).   Score ☐

Reaction to Gaining Freedom

Attempts to Return to Handler score (3), Runs off
Cheerfully (2), Slinks Away Cowed (1).   Score ☐

Interaction in Play Behaviour

Bullying and Possessive score (4), Boisterous and
Non-Aggressive (3), Playful but Submissive to
Others (2), Will not Play (1).   Score ☐

Feeding Behaviour

Greedy and Pushing score (3), Eats Steadily (2),
Reluctant and Easily Diverted (1).   Score ☐

                                  TOTAL SCORE ☐

Score 20 – 27:   Dominant puppy
Score 12 – 20:   Good average puppy
Below 12:   Submissive and sly

Fig. 8. Puppy Socialisation Test.

Puppy on Covered Table

Sharp Noise
Interested score (3), Little Response (2), Panic (1).
                                                    Score ☐

Hold Up Front Feet
Struggles score (2), Submits (1).   Score ☐

Hold Up Back Feet
Struggles score (2), Submits (1).   Score ☐

Stare Steadily Into Eyes
Holds Gaze score (3), Plays (2), Subdued (1).
                                                    Score ☐

Human Makes Growling Noise
Growls Back (3), Amused (2), Afraid (1).   Score ☐

Hold on Back for 30 seconds
Struggles score (3), Tolerates (2), Afraid (1). Score ☐

Hold Down Head and Rump
Score as above.   Score ☐

Open Mouth
Score as above.   Score ☐

Praise and Note Reaction
Resents (3), Pleased (2), Afraid (1).   Score ☐

Gently Pull Tail
Resents score (3), Tolerates (2), Cries (1).   Score ☐

                                        TOTAL SCORE ☐

Score 24 – 28:   Dominant puppy, may be difficult
                 to manage
Score 15 – 23:   Good average companion dog
                 material
Below 14:   Submissive, nervous.

Fig. 9. **Puppy Handling Test.**

Fig. 10. Test Handling of puppies.
Above: Hold the puppy up and stare into its eyes. The puppy should not resist.
Below: Turn the puppy on to its back, the well adjusted puppy will not struggle.

you in expense and worry later on. Of course, problems may become evident later which do not show at this time, but a pre-purchase health check is a good investment, and you can, at this time, get veterinary advice about worming and the preventative vaccination programme.

Having advised a veterinary check, it must be said it is not easy to arrange. It is understandable that the breeder is not going to be very happy at the removal of a puppy from her care "on approval" with the possibility of the puppy encountering disease, or traumatic happenings. The answer may be to ask a veterinary surgeon to call at the breeder's premises to check the puppy, but house calls are very expensive these days. If it proves most convenient to ask the breeder's veterinary surgeon to do the check, you can rest assured that the veterinary surgeon's verdict will be absolutely impartial. For future reference, a certificate of good health at the time of examination and suitability for the purpose for which you require the dog should be signed by the veterinary surgeon.

Preparations at Home

In view of the enormous amount of justifiable anger felt when footpaths, grass verges, parks and public places are soiled by dog excreta, you will be training your puppy to pass urine and faeces within your own garden as much as possible. Walks should be for exercise and not bowel-emptying outings. You have to decide how you will keep your own garden clean. Solid faeces should be picked up as soon as possible after excretion, using a couple of implements and bucket. A garden hoe and a coal shovel work well, but specially designed "grabs" may be bought through the dog newspapers. The excreta from one dog is best put down the household sewage system, either in a WC or by lifting a manhole cover. It is also possible to buy plastic bins which, filled with chemical, destroy solid excreta. The place from which the dog mess was picked up may be dusted with disinfectant powder, or dug over.

You have also to agree within the family in which rooms the puppy is to be allowed, whether it may sit on any furniture at all, whether it may go upstairs when it is safe to allow it to do so. It should be pointed out to those likely to transgress that it is cruel to secretly indulge a puppy by allowing it on the settee, for instance, when no-one else is looking. Treats of this kind only bring the puppy punishment later on, and also confuse its mind. Sometimes a person with an insecure outlook themselves will indulge the puppy believing it will then care for them more, but this is not true in practice, since dogs are conditioned to give their affection and respect to the pack leader responsible for discipline.

It is quite possible to convey to the puppy within a few weeks of having it in your home that it may never set foot on carpeted areas, or may never go upstairs. Later, when the puppy is adult, indulgences may be allowed occasionally, although the dog may feel so guilty about taking advantage of the offer that it really has no pleasure from the treat. In old age, or after illness, indulgences will be more frequent and are gratefully accepted. It follows that if your puppy is forbidden the carpeted sitting room, then members of the family must expect to spend some time, especially during the evenings, in the rooms in which it is allowed, otherwise you are shutting the dog out from the pack and that may be taken as a punishment.

When you have a new puppy in the home, it is very important to perfect a "front door drill" which all the family will follow. It is so easy for a puppy to slip out towards a road when the front door is opened to callers. The best routine is, no matter how great the urgency, to shut the puppy into the kitchen before you open a main door, and do it *always*.

Feeding the Puppy

The breeder should give you a diet sheet for the puppy. Be sure to obtain just the right foods, and the same quality of milk, because the puppy should be kept on exactly the same things it has been used to for at least two weeks. It has enough new experiences coming without changes in food. All meals should be given at room temperature, not straight from the refrigerator, but they are probably more appetising warmed. Just as much care must be taken with the puppy's food and milk and utensils as you would with a human baby's. The puppy is just as much subject to digestive upsets caused by bacteria colonising stale food or soiled dishes. Water should be always available.

Collection

Collect the puppy on a day when all the family are going to be at home but when nothing else important is happening. Mid-morning makes a good time, with the object of feeding the mid-day meal when you arrive home. Assuming that you will collect the puppy in a car, take someone who is willing to hold the puppy on their lap for this first ride. The puppy will feel more secure and is not then likely to develop phobias about car riding. Take a couple of towels for the puppy to sit on, and a cardigan to wrap around it for cosiness. If the puppy should urinate or vomit on this journey, it will not be a great disaster and no notice should be taken beyond cleaning the puppy up. The puppy should be talked to a little on the journey but not over-fussed, and there should be no visits made and no picnics which involve getting out of the car, as un-vaccinated puppies should not be put down until they get back to their own garden. Get home as quickly as you reasonably can, DO NOT take the puppy to the nearest hostelry to wet its head or anything like that!

Check List before bringing puppy home

1. Decide areas of home puppy is to use, and garden area where you will encourage excretion.
2. Check garden fence, and keep repair material available (pups will find gaps you have overlooked). Ensure gates latch securely.
3. Reposition all trailing electricity leads, telephone cords which puppy may bite.
4. Cover sandpits, you do not want these used as lavatories, and cover and fence deep ponds and swimming pools.
5. Remove household and garden chemicals, especially the very poisonous slug pellets which are very attractive to dogs, to absolutely safe storage.
6. Make children aware of the danger of leaving plastic toys and underwear accessible, plastic and nylon hosiery material swallowed by dogs is the cause of many surgical emergencies.
7. Arrange front door drill and make sure everyone knows about it.
8. Decide on a refuge to which dog can retreat.

Check List of Supplies required before bringing puppy home

1. Supply of food exactly in accordance with breeder's menu.
2. Gripewater (as for human babies) for hiccups and minor digestive troubles. Liquid paraffin is also very useful.
3. Water bowl, food dish.
4. Hide chews (small size are best liked) and very large marrow bone.
5. Disinfectant for floors . . . diluted household bleach best, and carpet cleaner.
6. Mild disinfectant correctly diluted for anything which is in direct contact with puppy.
7. Bed . . . cardboard cartons are best for first few months.
8. Bedding, polyester fur laid on newspaper, a soft material (to wrap round puppy if liked). Preferably not an old garment.
9. Picking-up tools and buckets for excreta.
10. Soft puppy collar and lead.
11. Vet's telephone number and breeder's too.
12. Hot water bottle and cover.

Section III

MANAGING YOUR PUPPY

9

SOCIALISATION TIME

THE modern method of managing your new puppy so that it integrates properly with your family and becomes a successful companion relies on recent discoveries about the way puppies learn and the phases of development which they go through.

The first twelve weeks of life are crucial in the puppy. For the first three weeks it will have been entirely dependent on its mother. From three weeks to twelve weeks the puppy goes through a very important socialisation period when all its attitudes to dogs, people and the outside world are being formed.

Socialisation with other dogs comes with awareness of the rest of the litter and continues until it is taken away to a new home. During this time the puppy learns how to play, how to defend itself and how to attack and generally to carry itself as a member of the canine race. It is a good thing for the puppy to have some interaction with other dogs throughout its life, but some have little opportunity for mixing once they have left the litter and yet they will still have a very good idea what being a dog is all about.

From three weeks until the time the puppy leaves the litter it is also learning to socialise with humans, first through the breeder and kennel assistants only, and later with people coming to see the litter with a view to buying. The puppy learns to recognise voices, faces and to appreciate handling, and learns to respond to actions made by humans . . . if a person bends down the puppy will come to them . . . the puppy will stand on its hind legs in the play pen, "asking" to be picked up etc. Between seven and fourteen weeks is the critical period for socialisation with humans. It is crucial to recognise and fully use this period of special susceptibility in order to fashion your puppy into an adaptable and well-rounded dog personality.

Mishandling during these socialisation periods can create problems that are difficult, possibly even impossible to erase later. An added difficulty is the effect of this mishandling may not be noticeable at first, but may be triggered later by some trauma or specific situation in adult life.

The particular problems that can arise are aggression and shyness or nervous habits. Puppies are especially impressionable between eight and twelve weeks of age, and an experience that produces acute fear at this time may "mark" a puppy for life, especially one which has already some hereditary tendency to nervousness or shyness. It is for this reason that managing the puppy during its first weeks in your home, so that it does the right things and has little opportunity to do wrong is so important to its future life. Hard punishment should be avoided at this time, and in this sense punishment includes leaving the puppy on its own to be lonely and frightened. The chart on page 79 will show that the puppy is not at this time capable of any calculated act which deserves punishment, beyond the word NO!

If you have obtained your puppy from a reputable breeder the canine socialisation will have taken place and the human socialisation will have been begun with tact and care, giving you good material with which to continue. The kennelised puppy which has not been handled or had "house" experience has bigger shocks to come when you take it into your home, so you have a harder task to face. It is important that you do not delay obtaining your puppy beyond the eight-week age, especially where bigger breeds are concerned, such as the German Shepherd Dogs, Rottweilers, Dobermans and Boxers which can tend to be dominant.

In practice this will mean that you almost certainly will have to pre-order from an expected litter. If the breeder has to retain dogs after eight weeks, then extra socialisation with more people should be deliberately given so that the puppy will not lack experience when it does go out to a home.

As the 8–12 week period is one in which the puppy

should not have any fear-provoking experiences, it is important that the puppy should not be left alone for more than three hours, except overnight, and it would be preferable if it was not left for as long as that. The natural instinct of an isolated animal, especially one which has so lately come from a "pack" is to try to escape by digging, and chewing, and drawing attention to its plight by crying and howling.

This is a natural protective move which serves a useful purpose in the wild and is not, at this stage, punishable behaviour, but if the puppy has occasion to use this escape behaviour often, because you leave it unreasonably long, then the behaviour pattern becomes imprinted and you will have a dog which can never be left without its destroying its surroundings.

The puppy so far has had all its needs supplied by its mother, its first pack leader. Later, the breeder assumes the pack leader rôle, supplying food, comfort and keeping away danger in whatever form it appears . . . such as breaking up too aggressive play. In order to give your puppy an atmosphere of security in which to adjust to life and grow into a confident well-balanced dog, you, the owner, must now assume the pack leader and provider rôle. Being a pack leader does not imply that you only dole out discipline, you protect and comfort too, and you order the puppy's life so that it is all enjoyable. Doing what the pack leader wants is a natural response, although there will be, as the puppy grows up, some degree of rebellion unless it is a very submissive character.

When your puppy accepts you as its protector and pack leader, you should see that, during the critical period for socialisation at 8 to 12 weeks, the puppy encounters as many types of people as possible, including women, men and children. The puppy should also at this time be "exposed" within your protection to a variety of experiences. Unfortunately, the puppy will not be able to walk out on the lead as the innoculation programme will not be completed until 12 or 14 weeks old, but you can carry your puppy down the High Street and let it hear traffic noise, whistles and hoots from within the safety of your arms,

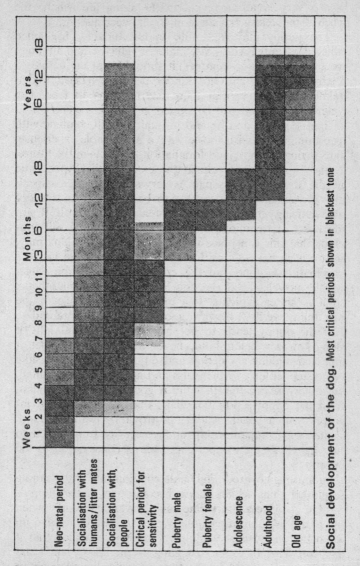

Fig. 11. Social development of the dog.
   Most critical periods shown in the blackest tone.

and a very important event in its young life will be the visit to the veterinary surgeon for its vaccinations.

The puppy may be, quite understandably, frightened when confronted with noise or large vehicles, and although you will be offering comfort, it should be in the nature of "jollying along" and not tender sympathy, because that reinforces the idea that there is something to fear. The veterinary surgeon will be skilled in handling animals and giving injections and he and his staff will all combine with you to make the visit to the vet's a pleasurable experience, thus laying down a good foundation for visits in the future. If the puppy should yelp at the entry of the hypodermic needle, the momentary pain is very soon forgotten, especially if you, the pack leader, are being bright and breezy and showing no apprehension or fear emotion at all. If you are upset or tremulous yourself, then the puppy will conclude that this is a place where fear is justified. You may, if you wish have a tiny food reward ready to give as the vaccination is done, but this could become a habit which will be unwelcome if the dog has to have an anaesthetic, so it is better avoided. Just make the visit "one of the nice things we do". Reward good behaviour, ignore bad.

If the puppy tends to be shy, ignore that and jolly it along towards being bold, never sympathise and pet it unless something accidental and unjust has happened, like being stepped on . . . then fuss and apology are warranted, but otherwise, assume that life is good and take care that, from the puppy's point of view, that it *is* good. This involves you as pack leader in providing warmth, food, shelter and companionship and a security from which to sum up all the new experiences life is releasing on to the puppy.

Submitting to grooming, nail clipping and ear cleaning is another thing which has to become part of the puppy's routine . . . give a short time each day and stop only when the puppy is submitting quietly, it is a mistake to give up when the puppy is struggling . . . it may conclude that it has *won.* Try not to let struggling occur. Praise, laugh and be happy afterwards, your tone of voice in all dealings with the puppy are very important. In these weeks you

may find that you are frequently obliged to praise, laugh
and be happy; will that be doing you good too? You may
find in the puppy a significant lift to your own spirits, and
it will be rewarding to see how well the puppy responds
to the teaching you provide.

In these early weeks when the puppy is being socialised
no punishments should be used, indeed, the puppy is not
capable of knowing about punishment yet. You will, of
course, sometimes have to deter the puppy from some
danger, and then the word NO is the most important in
your vocabulary. Say it very sharply, and rather loudly
and make sure it is obeyed by ceasing the action the
puppy was making. At this stage, follow the NO with a
diversion of some kind to interest the puppy in something
else, just as you would a very young child. Unfortunately,
we cannot reason with puppies and say, "don't touch that,
it is sharp or hot . . ." We can only get into the dog's mind
that there are some objects, some areas, utterly forbidden
to it.

10

THE PRINCIPLES OF LEARNING

ALTHOUGH we have said that dogs can learn by classical
conditioning, the ringing of a bell bringing the conditioned
response, salivation and readiness for a meal, this is not
the main way that the dog in our home learns how to
behave. Far more important is what the scientists call
"instrumental conditioning", and this means, in simple
language, "the action brings its own reward". Dogs learn
as a result of doing things, and the keynote of our system
in dog management is to let the dog learn from doing the
right things, not to have to unlearn the wrong ones.

We have a certain amount of difficulty in communi-
cating with dogs because they have no language and
because they cannot link a current action with an event
that occurred some time ago. A dog can only establish
the rightness of its action if it is congratulated or rewarded
or punished tangibly within two or three seconds of the

action being performed. This is why correction of misdeeds is so difficult. In colloquial terms, the dog just cannot understand "what you are on about" if the misdeed hapten, twenty, minutes ago. You may say that your dog has a sense of guilt, "he knows when he has done wrong", but this is a reaction to your face, your tone of voice, in fact, if you always come in raging at the mess in the kitchen your dog may have a permanent guilt complex whenever you come home.

The "reward" learning method works in this way: You want your dog to lie down, so every time he does so, you immediately say the word "Down", praise him or give a delicious food reward. After a very short time the dog will make the association and will lie down in anticipation of being praised or getting something to eat . . . just as Berry, the Boxer, rolls on her back to trigger this reaction in her owner.

Because the dog soon finds that its action has a positive reinforcement, that is, it "pays off" according to the dog's outlook, the dog will tend to repeat the action, and it has learnt to do one thing which you want.

Give the dog a verbal cue by saying "Sit", showing once or twice the position you mean by that hissing *S-i-i-i-t* sound, and when the dog drops into that position, you reward it immediately. The dog will soon make the association between the hissing sound and the need to fold up its back legs so that it receives the reward in a body position which pleases its pack leader. It has been found that to be most effective the reward must be given within half a second of the dog making the right response. Berry was taught to sit in ten minutes after dinner one night by calling her and giving her one broad bean every time she dropped into the sit position. Alas, she vomited all over the carpet afterwards, broad beans not being the most suitable puppy food but the thing most handy at the time. She has never forgotten what sit means, in fact she seems to feel that "sit" should bring her a round of applause every time!

Of course, the value of the reward and the motivation the dog feels to do the action varies . . . a tired, sleepy puppy, with a tummy full after a good meal may be very slow to respond to "Sit" even with the certainty of a reward.

If the reward stops coming . . . that is, if Berry continually rolls on to her back soliciting play and praise, but her owner is too preoccupied with work to notice her, then she will assume this attitude less often, and eventually give it up altogether . . . it has ceased to "pay off" as far as she is concerned. This is called "extinction" of a behaviour pattern.

If Berry is noticed when she does her rolling trick, quite often, but not always, this supplies her with an incentive to try harder, to do it more often to see if she is going to be lucky this time, and so, once a dog has learned a piece of behaviour (or a trick), rewards should be given only from time to time at varying intervals. The same principle applies when people play fruit machines, there just might be a reward coming at the next pull of the handle.

These two methods, regular reward and then intermittent reward, are the secret behind much of the training of police and army dogs which perform such useful service, sometimes perfecting far more intricate tasks than is generally known. The same ploys may be used to train dogs out of bad habits they have acquired.

Punishment does have its place (but not with puppies of under about three months old). An appropriate punishment can be effective in older puppies and adults, but like the reward, it must happen immediately the offence is committed, and it must be applied consistently and fairly. Losing one's temper, punishing too hard too late, and for something which the dog cannot understand, is ugly, and it does nothing to get you a more obedient dog. It may get you a cringing one, or it may get you a resentful one, but not a good one.

The problem with applying punishment is the possibility of creating anxiety and causing aggression feelings in the dog. Punishment must be of sufficient strength the first time it is used to disrupt the unwanted behaviour but not so strong as to frighten the dog and to shake its faith in its pack leader. Punishment must never be prolonged.

A big dog will punish another, by jumping on its back and rubbing the offender's nose in the mud. Honour then being satisfied, both parties get up and walk away and an hour after are curled up together in the same bed. It would be very difficult for us to punish a dog in that way . . . we could not expect to be quick enough or accurate enough, we might get hurt in the process, or the whole thing might turn into a game and therefore become a reward. By the time we had reached for a weapon, the dog might not make the correct association of deed with reaction.

Both authors of this book have found that the magic punishment is by far the most effective. The thrown object which strikes the dog while it is actually committing the crime is a punishment which acts as a great deterrent while not really hurting the dog at all, its unexpected arrival being the secret of its potency. When Anna, the Doberman, was young, she enjoyed making raids on the handbag of the lady of the house. In order to stop this happening we set up a trap; we deliberately left the bag in a suitable place, and having armed ourselves with a bean bag, we waited until Anna put her nose in the handbag, and then, wham! Something sped through the air and landed on Anna's rear, inflicting immediate punishment although no humans were visible and no-one shouted. Dogs watch their humans so much that they can predict many of our actions and the most agile of us are so much clumsier than dogs so they get a lot of warning about what we are going to do . . . but the invisibly thrown object is *unpredictable* and anything which takes the dog by surprise makes a very strong impression. Handbags are quite safe from Anna now, and this remedy could be used again in other circumstances. We once had a kennels situated in an old orchard . . . little apples broke up many behaviour patterns there with our Boxers!

A child's water pistol is another "magic" weapon which can be used to disturb an animal committing a crime . . . very effective if used from an upstairs window too. None of these things *hurt* and they are not degrading to the owner, as physical violence can be, and if cleverly done, the dog will not associate the owner with the action at all. The thrown object also serves as a distraction, even if it misses the dog, by the time it has investigated that, the sequence of behaviour is broken up and may not be started again.

Punishment by objects which the dog is actually in the

Fig. 12. The booby trap in action.

act of attacking works very well too . . . the dog so nimble with its paws that it can open cupboards will never trust that cupboard again if a carefully devised "booby trap" of a pile of tins falls out next time. These "magic" deterrents are much more effective even than hitting the dog as it opens the cupboard, if you should be lucky enough to see the deed being done. It is probably the surprise element when the dog feels itself to be unobserved, and the lack of any preliminary movement or warning which does the trick. If the booby trap could somehow be wired to a sound recording of the owner's voice, that would probably represent the ultimate in the unexpected.

Ignoring the dog and the withdrawal of attention and petting can also be a punishment, effective in the long term when a dog is dominating or bullying one member of the family. The ploy should be for all the rest of the humans to turn off the dog completely, never letting even the eyes rest upon it, while the dominated or bullied person provides all food, walks, and other forms of comfort or indulgence. The dog then *has* to turn to that person. This regime works well, provided all the family co-operate and never forget that they are not supposed to be relating to the dog at all over this rehabilitation period.

Putting the dog into solitary confinement can be counterproductive to your purpose and it is quite inadvisable in young puppies during the socialisation period. The problem is that the dog may not make the association between "solitary" and crime and the next time you leave the dog when you are going out, it may assume that the last thing it did before you shut the door upon it was a "crime" . . . a pity if this was going into the garden to be clean!

These principles of learning are those you will use from the time you get your puppy. The punishments will, if needed, come into use after the puppy is three months old when the puppy is capable of knowing right from wrong and your relationship with the little dog is firmly established.

11

HOUSETRAINING

THE chart on page 88 shows the comparison between the puppy and the human infant, and may help you to be tolerant of the puppy's failings when young, especially when you consider how very much more patient we have to be with human babies.

Gestation time in the bitch is short, and her puppies have to be equipped to fend for themselves very early in life, in case, in the wild dog, their mother should be killed. Born with ears and eyes undeveloped, within a month of birth the puppy can see, hear and stand. At eight weeks it can run and play constructively with its littermates, it will move away from the nest to urinate and defecate, and it will never urinate during sleep. The puppy can run towards a person who attracts its attention, and it is beginning to learn to associate sounds with action you require it to take. The brain capacity is developing towards acquiring knowledge about the world in which it is to live. At the age of eight weeks the puppy can achieve far more in every way than a human baby.

The puppy can control bladder and bowel movement for a few minutes at eight weeks old but it cannot convey the necessity to humans, unless they are watching the instinctive and quite identifiable movements the puppy makes before the act. Fairly reliable control is reached in the puppy from the age of four months, and 95 per cent. of puppies will be entirely reliable by the age of eight months, a state which we do not expect in the human infant until three or four years, perhaps as old as six years. Elimination control will relax during illness, such as an episode of loose bowel movements, extreme agitation or, of course, being unable to get outside to be clean, but this restriction will also apply to a child up to six years or even beyond. We have in the puppy considerably less nuisance over toilet training than we do in our own young, so it seems unreasonable to lose patience with a puppy for "dirtiness" when our own species are completely uncontrolled, and in a far more labour-intensive way, for at least five times as long!

There have been cases of newly acquired puppies being rejected within a few days because they are "messing all over the house". This excuse, for that is what it is, reflects badly only on those that make it. The puppy should not be "all over the house". It should be restricted to those areas where there are people to watch it, preferably on uncarpeted floors, and the puppy's elimination needs

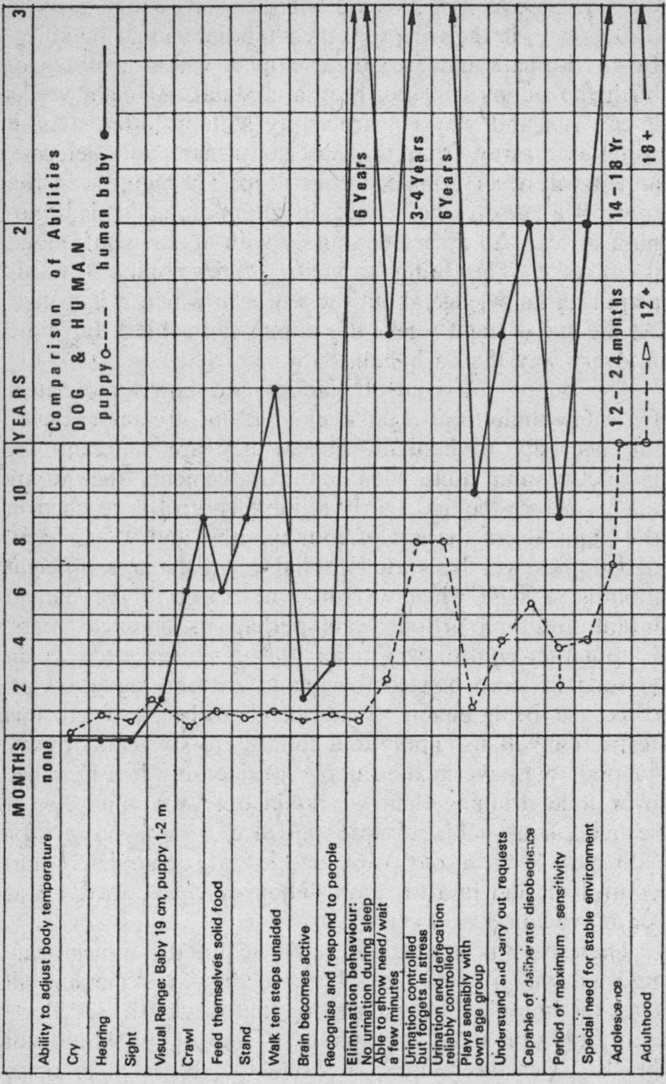

Comparison of Abilities
DOG & HUMAN
puppy o——— ● human baby

MONTHS	2	4	6	8	10	1 YEARS	2	3

Ability to adjust body temperature — none

Cry

Hearing

Sight

Visual Range: Baby 19 cm, puppy 1-2 m

Crawl

Feed themselves solid food

Stand

Walk ten steps unaided

Brain becomes active

Recognise and respond to people

Elimination behaviour:
No urination during sleep
Able to show need/wait a few minutes — 6 Years

Urination controlled but forgets in stress — 3-4 Years

Urination and defecation reliably controlled — 6 Years

Plays sensibly with own age group

Understand and carry out requests

Capable of deliberate disobedience

Period of maximum · sensitivity

Special need for stable environment

Adolescence — 12 – 24 months / 14 – 18 Yr

Adulthood — 12+ / 18+

Fig. 13. Comparison of abilities chart.

should be anticipated. In puppies, as in babies, feeding and elimination follow each other very quickly, so you must be ready to take the puppy outside the *instant* it has finished eating. As puppies do not urinate during sleep after 2½ weeks old, you will need to be ready when the puppy wakes. Agitation and being left alone, or crying, will certainly make the puppy pass urine.

You will notice that during play, the puppy will sniff around the floor in a tight circle, probably assuming a worried expression, when it has the urge to eliminate, but the interval between *indication* and *doing* is very short. If you are busy or preoccupied the puppy may soil the floor and it can be very difficult to be alert all the time when you are cooking or talking on the telephone. The time between indication and elimination gets longer with age, as it does with a child, and the puppy at 4–5 months will give you a much clearer signal, progressing to actual "asking" in some very plain fashion to go out. They usually stare at the door, or bang at it with their paws. Berry, the Boxer, will press down on the door handle and let herself out, the height of sophisticated training. This was a trick she discovered for herself, which has been subsequently reinforced by reward.

Adult dogs and bitches normally last for several hours without urinating (unless they are territory marking). In summer when doors are standing open, you have no occasion to think of the dog's needs, except perhaps first thing in the morning and late at night. In winter, the fully housetrained dog can be asked to go into the garden . . . "to be good" and it will then eliminate on command, provided you reward it as noted before when it performs.

The word or phrase you use for housetraining must be decided when you get the puppy and it must then be used every time the act is performed in the right place. It is quite hard to find a word that is acceptable to use in public and one which will not be used in any other context. Generations of Boxers have responded to "go and be good" although they know that "she is so *good*" is a universal form of praise, which, when used indoors, does not cause the fountain to flow. It is the sound and inflection which dogs recognise and not the actual words. "Outside", or "go and be clean" are other acceptable phrases for housetraining. Anna, the Doberman, will urinate at the sound of an undulating whistle, a refined signal indeed.

With your newly acquired puppy, you will have to go out into the garden, and *stay with the puppy*, repeating your chosen phrase over and over until the puppy performs, when you will congratulate it most enthusiastically. By the association technique, the puppy will eventually connect the doing with the phrase, and later, you can fling the door wide and use the phrase, and the dog will go out to eliminate without delay. While you may, to a large extent, leave your adult to take care of its own needs, it is extremely useful to keep the phrase within the dog's memory, so that if you are away from home, or on a car journey, you can ask your dog to do the necessary and get results very quickly even on strange ground.

We have said that the puppy will indicate that it is going to pass urine and that you have a very short time in which to get it outside. Puppies have very little power of concentration, like toddlers, and once in the garden, the puppy may look at the flowers or chase a butterfly, quite forgetting what the mission was all about. Staying with the puppy takes patience on your part, but there is no way to avoid this part of the management. Keep an umbrella handy by the door, but take as comfort that thousands and thousands of other new puppy owners are also walking the garden in their pyjamas in the dawn hours. Turning the young puppy out on its own is quite useless; as the door shuts upon it, the puppy's whole attention turns to getting back inside with the rest of the household pack.

If you have acquired a very young puppy in a small breed during bad weather, you may feel that you do not wish to take your puppy out into the cold. In this case, as the breeder will almost certainly use newspaper to cover the floor of the playpen in which the puppies were reared, you may continue to train your puppy to use newspaper, perhaps in a conservatory, or near the back door, but not over the whole floor. This is not ideal as, eventually, newspaper is going to be wrong and the garden is going to be right, but in some cases it may be advisable to keep the puppy indoors. When the time comes to make the transition to outside, you will have to take the puppy out and stay with it, as advised earlier, and it helps to move a piece of used newspaper out to the spot in the garden where you wish the elimination behaviour to take place.

12

THE FIRST DAY IN YOUR HOME

YOUR relationship with your puppy starts to be made the minute the breeder puts it into your arms. Your aim is to make this little animal a happy subordinate in the family and each human in the pack must work out a relationship with the dog. Consistency as individuals and as a family is the keynote. Young children are sometimes delighted to have a pack member below them in the family. They will quickly try to order the puppy about and to administer punishments, probably the same kind of slaps which they receive themselves. They may also call the puppy at inappropriate times and generally produce a confusion in the mind of the puppy which will hamper your management.

A definite demarcation line should be established between those family members who may manage and train the puppy, and those who may not. Close observation should always be kept on games involving little children and young dogs, lest either side is becoming over-excited or unwisely treated. Parents should make it quite clear to children that the puppy is not a mechanical toy; it must always be left undisturbed when it goes into its box to sleep and it must always be handled with consideration and commonsense. It is not unknown to find that children and their friends are teaching the puppy to jump low hurdles or ropes. Great fun indeed, but not a good idea when the puppy is able to jump over the garden fence.

"See what they are doing and stop them doing it" is perhaps an out-dated maxim for those caring for children, but not at all a bad idea when you have children and young dogs playing together.

There are a few general rules about new puppies which it is advisable to observe, in order that there shall not be the slightest health risk to humans or dog.

1. Never let the dog eat from plates used by the family, always feed it in its own bowl.

2. Pick up and dispose of the dog's excreta as soon as possible after it has been passed.

3. All the family should wash their hands after handling the puppy and before eating or preparing food.

4. Because of the small, but significant risk of infection by puppy roundworm (toxocara canis), be extra careful that children's faces and hands are washed frequently and always before sleep, or eating. Puppy roundworm is not the same as, or the cause of, the very prevalent *threadworms* in children.

5. Try to discourage the puppy from licking children.

Your puppy, having travelled happily in your arms from the breeder's premises, will be ready to urinate immediately you reach your home, so carry it straight to the part of the garden you mean to use, put it down, and say your urination phrase over and over again. Many people think it would be best if the puppy used the bottom of the garden, well out of the way, but remember, you will be going as well, in bad weather, late at night and early, and you have no time to change into outdoor shoes, so you may decide it would be prudent to use a patch near the house.

You should, this first time, have an easy success, because the need will be already there, so when the puppy has performed, praise it and pet it as if it had just won a gold medal, and then bring it indoors. This would be a good time to offer a small drink, and then to let the puppy spend half an hour exploring the kitchen without too much human interference. This will be a big landmark in the puppy's development; it may be the first time it has been outside of a playpen, it will be the first time it has been without its litter mates, and there will be a whole lot of huge skyscraper objects to be looked at, smelt and assessed.

You may find the puppy tends to get behind or under furniture. This may not be through fear, but because the strength of the general lighting is too strong. Young puppies avoid strong daylight for some weeks after they can see quite well in subdued light.

Puppies may also be nervous of wind and blowing trees at first, and also of the sound of your household appliances which may have a different note to the ones used by the breeder. Children must be taught that it is cruel to make loud sounds, or hissing sounds, right into the puppy's ear, or to startle the puppy in any way. As the dog grows older, mistreatment of this kind may precipitate an attack on the child which, while regrettable, will not be strictly the dog's fault. Because the dog's reaction to mistreatment is so instinctive and instant, it should be easy for a child to understand that teasing in any form is forbidden.

Unfortunately, many adults know no other form of play than teasing and this is a pity, particularly with a sensitive puppy. In the early days, the puppy must have a fair chance in any game that is played, and it should be allowed to win little contests, but never big ones. You must decide when playtime is over. The puppy must always allow handling, and always give up a "prize" to an adult human. It is not wise to allow little children to take things from a possessive dog.

After the puppy has explored for a while it should be fed, in accordance with the breeder's instructions. Take it outside again immediately to be clean and follow the procedure as before. The puppy should be ready for a sleep in the warmly-lined carton you have prepared for it in a cosy corner in the kitchen . . . check for draughts at the floor level. Be ready to take the puppy out again when it wakes from sleep, and so the routine goes on through the day . . . we did say you needed plenty of free time! But in a short while you will have won, provided you manage to avoid accidents occurring.

Naming the puppy is an immediate necessity, for you will want to use the name at every possible opportunity to get it embedded in the puppy's mind. A short crisp name which all the family can pronounce in the same way is ideal. Rover, the favourite dog name in Edwardian times, has gone completely out of use now that it is anti-social and dangerous for dogs to wander outside their owner's premises. Pick up the puppy, look straight into its face and say, "you are Pixie," or whatever name has been chosen. Use the name when the puppy is coming towards you, when you put its food down, and when you are playing, so that the puppy has every chance to get to know its "signal". In the first few hours in your home the puppy has begun learning to use the garden for toilet purposes, and begun learning its name, two very big steps towards maturity.

Remembering what the puppy's background has been, it is very useful if you can stay in the room where it is sleeping, keeping busy on tasks, of course, but within sight if the puppy should stir. You can sing or have the radio on if you wish, absolute quiet is by no means necessary, but good humour, light and bright voices are. Men with lugubrious grave voices might even make an effort to raise theirs above growl level.

13

THE FIRST NIGHT

THE day which for all the family has been so exciting will eventually wind down to bedtime. Because it is so important to reinforce the pack leader's role of protector and comforter before you become a disciplinarian also, and because most of us regard cleanliness within the house of prime importance, if you are so inclined take the puppy and its box into your bedroom and put it beside the bed, so that you can be within touch of the puppy all night.

The traditional way is to leave the puppy downstairs safely tucked up in its cardboard box with a well covered warm hot water bottle and possibly a clock to resemble its mother's heartbeat. You may have to endure some crying and go down during the night to comfort it but if the puppy has been well fed and allowed to relieve itself last thing it should sleep peacefully most of the night. But be prepared to be up early.

By taking the puppy to your bedroom you do not form a habit for a lifetime. You can always begin to train the puppy to the kitchen in two or three weeks' time, when it has confidence in you and your surroundings, when it understands NO and its name. The puppy is *not* going to be unhygienically on or in your bed, it is going to be in a high-sided cardboard carton, close enough for you to put out a hand to comfort the puppy if it should cry. When the puppy stirs and wants to urinate, at first light probably, you can be aware and able to take the puppy outside, so there is no set-back to housetraining. There is also no set-back to your relationship, because the puppy has not experienced any distress or fear during this sensitive time.

Even with their littermates in a playpen, puppies do not urinate and mess all night. They do so after their last meal, and then, unless they are disturbed, the playpen will remain clean until the puppies get up, at first light or when the noises start outside. They then perform very promptly indeed, but if you have your puppy in the bedroom, you will not run the risk of "mess all over the carpet". Cover it with plastic if you must while you prove the fact for yourself.

Last year, when ten Boxer puppies went to individual new homes, ten new owners (mostly the male half of the partnership), slept with one shoulder out of bed and their hand on the puppy for some hours of the night. Both puppy and owner benefited, because it is a human attribute to be more proud of and to feel more affection for a little animal that you have had to care for. It is a good idea to let the adults share in the care of the puppy in this way and for it not to monopolise, or be monopolised by, any one person.

If there is an insurmountable barrier to taking the puppy into the bedroom for a week or two, there is no objection to a member of the family having a bed in the kitchen with the puppy. The result will be just the same, companionship, touch-comfort, and continuation of house training.

Some very discerning parents were willing to follow out the bedroom routine for the new puppy, but realised a tiny stirring of jealousy in their two little boys, who regarded sleeping in the parents' room as a very great privilege. Knowing that an early jealousy of the puppy would not be productive to a good relationship, the two little boys were allowed to bring their sleeping bags into the parents' room, and the puppy went into its box. They had a sort of dormitory arrangement for a few days, but none of the elements in the family had hurt or lonely feelings so the minimal upset in arrangements was wholly worthwhile.

14

THE NEXT FEW WEEKS

THE puppy's first full day in your home begins with going outside again, being praised for action, being called by its name when it is approaching already, and by the word NO when it is advancing on anything which is to be forbidden.

The four or five meals advised by the breeder should be served at regular times and have water always available, even if the puppy is having milky meals. The puppy should be wakened for meals but not for any other purpose, as it requires a lot of sleep. Take the opportunity to stand the puppy on a covered table for a few seconds, gradually increasing the time, to prepare for the day when the veterinary surgeon will want to examine it, and begin the grooming routine, even if the puppy has very little coat to comb at this age. If the puppy has the type of coat to be bathed often, start the use of a hair-dryer early in life.

The puppy will be going on with its exploring and having new experiences, and being handled by new people as friends come to see your lovely puppy. As the puppy gets to regard its box as its home, it will be useful to leave it for a short while, even ten minutes, while you go into another room, so that the puppy begins to have the experience of being alone; your return should be cheerful, not too sympathetic even if the puppy is crying, but at this stage, you should not allow the puppy to cry for very long. Never give the puppy the impression that it has only to squeak to bring you running, puppies will quickly learn to exploit that. Praise the puppy if it has been good, ignore other behaviour at this stage.

Keep before you the maxim that the puppy is not to be distressed or unhappy; there are plenty of pleasing distractions you can offer to keep it amused. There are many toys for dogs available to be bought; beware of those with squeakers inside as a strong puppy will get them out and they may be swallowed with dire results.

Rawhide chews are very popular, and less messy than bones, and a quoit ring gives a lot of fun. Some things, such as a strong polythene bucket, amuse the puppy very well and are safe to play with provided they are removed when it becomes possible to swallow pieces of the material.

It is usual to say that it is unwise to give old shoes and gloves, or pieces of cotton cloth to pull, as the puppy cannot distinguish between these discarded things and good ones. This is a valid theory, but when there is so much mileage to be got from an old leather shoe in terms of dog-play, and we need to give them a variety of interests and activities, it seems a pity to consign a good play object straight to the dustbin. We may also be crediting the dog with too much discernment, if we allow a hide chew, but not a hide glove or shoe . . . the shape and colour look very different to us, but we really do not know how they look to a puppy.

With Anna, we did not feel confident enough to take the chance of giving clothing or shoes as our boys are always liable to leave good garments lying around, even in the garden. We elected to give her three things only, a football, a cricket ball and a hardwood log. She has never chewed on anything else or chewed any item of clothing, although the log is now down to an almost round ball of wood through prolonged chewing on it.

You can teach a dog what is permitted by giving used clothing as toys only in certain locations. A shoe given to the dog and kept in the garden or the kitchen is a toy;

shoes and gloves in the bedroom must not be touched. And if a new pair of shoes should be left in the kitchen? Sorry, but that is your fault! Berry has been one of the hardest and most destructive dogs encountered in a whole lifetime of dog keeping, but although she sleeps in our bedroom and is now of an age when she can get out of her box and walk around during the night if she wishes, she has never touched any article of clothing in the bedroom, although old shoes, and pieces of cotton cloth are part of her toy collection.

It is not a bad thing to live by the maxim NO DOG OR PUPPY EVER COMMITS ANY CRIME. The bad episodes happen because people ALLOWED THEM TO HAPPEN, either by sins of omission . . . not supervising the dog, or leaving it alone unreasonably long, or by sins of commission, leaving precious articles where the dog can get at them. Not shutting doors to sitting rooms and bedrooms can be a major crime in a puppy-owning home, and being untidy is just as bad. Perfection in humans and dogs is impossible to obtain, and there will be some teeth marked objects during puppy days, but it is really up to the family to see that damage is minimal. You cannot be promised that all the joy a dog will bring your family will not be balanced in a small way by some losses, but with care and forethought the damage should be minimal.

Since it is very difficult to keep an eye on the puppy at all times through the day, there are bound to be some puddles on the floor, but if the puppy is kept on a newspaper covered surface, the cleaning should be quite easy. Do wash up all mistakes, preferably with diluted bleach, as a pine disinfectant seems to accentuate the smell of urine, and puppies will return to the same spot again and again. Every act of elimination done outside on command is a step towards housetraining, every one inside the house is a step back and it is really up to the owner to determine which way progress shall go.

If you must leave the puppy for an hour or so, you must expect that it will have needed to pass urine or faeces, and there must be NO PUNISHMENT . . . what alternative would a young creature, human or animal have? As the puppy grows up, you may express a little disapproval as you clean up, to show that you are not overjoyed to have to do this, but if the puppy could not get out, if there was no-one to ask, then there can be no blame. Pulling the puppy over to the mess, or the really primitive "rubbing his nose in it", gives you a puppy with a dirty, smelly face, and nothing more. Remember, toddlers make similar messes for very much longer, even when people are with them constantly, so have patience with your puppy. Dogs are very quickly and easily housetrained if they have the opportunity to make their needs known.

During the first week it is a good idea to let the puppy wear a soft collar for a few minutes each day . . . it will scratch at the collar, but in the end it will become a habit to wear it. Anna now feels undressed without her collar and shows anxiety when it is removed. Later, attach a leash and let it trail behind the puppy. As you pass, pick it up occasionally, and let the puppy walk a few steps "on the lead" before letting go again, so that it has some idea of feeling control by the lead before more formal training begins.

While your puppy is tiny, you should pick it up frequently, and let other responsible adults do so as well. The puppy is not allowed to struggle, it should not be put down until it is quiet in the holder's arms, and it is a good idea to ask responsible people to put a comb through the coat, turn back the ears, and to go through other movements so that the puppy is not orientated to handling in this way by only one person.

During the first week it is a good idea to take the puppy for short trips in the car, even a deliberate ride to the end of the road and back to reinforce car travel in its mind. Hold the puppy in the arms at first, later on it should go on the back seat, or for a small breed, in a wire crate if it is customary to use one in the breed. Dog guards, confining the dog to the back end of estate cars are very fashionable, and are particularly necessary if there are several children to occupy the seats, but if there is a shunting-type crash, the dog takes the impact first. Crates are also being used in cars increasingly often, even for big dogs, but the dog is then restricted in room and also ventilation, and it cannot move to the shady side of the car in hot weather. It is better to have your dog trained to behave well than to buy expensive apparatus to keep it in.

Do not forget the praise when the dog has done well, with or without the food reward. It is all too easy to say nothing when the dog fulfils your wish, but to remonstrate volubly when it does not, and we all know what a word of praise does for our own egos.

When giving food rewards, have a care to the total dietary intake; you could be giving the dog something close to double rations if you reward it often. A crumb of sweet biscuit, the smallest scrap of cheese rewards a puppy; beware of using vitaminised preparations too heavily; it is harmful to give more than the manufacturer's recommendations.

When the puppy is completely at home in your house, but not on the day it is being wormed or has had vaccinations, you can, if you intend to, start the puppy sleeping in the kitchen. Make sure the little dog is tired when it goes to bed. It will be, by now, familiar with the room and the bed, and if you make it cosy with a hot water bottle, it should go down without fuss, and remain quiet until early morning, when you will have to try to hear the lark first, in order to save the puppy making a puddle and going back on the early housetraining. Some dogs are of much more independent natures than others; some will not mind being alone, others will feel it keenly, and in such case, if the puppy is no trouble while it is with you, you may decide to leave the sleeping arrangements as they began. Later in its life, it makes sense to have a dog which can protect the vulnerable parts of the house rather than one shut in the kitchen, not usually very rewarding territory for burglars.

There are an increasing number of cases being reported of dogs being poisoned by fumes from solid fuel boilers when shut in kitchens and utility rooms overnight. Make sure the puppy's sleeping place is ventilated.

When your puppy is firmly established in your home and is confident and happy, then is the time to begin on the basic obedience training which will make your dog acceptable anywhere. The usual basic commands are Sit, Down, Stay, Come and Heel, but any words that you choose are acceptable. There should be no confusion between the words and the action wanted. Having taught a dog to "lie" on the command "down", it is all too easy to say "down" when you want it to stop jumping up, and besides producing confusion, it is unrealistic to think that a bouncing dog is going to "lie down". So you lost that round . . . don't lose too many! NO is useful for many acts of wrongdoing.

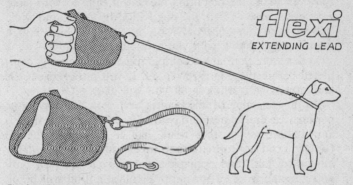

Fig. 14. "Flexi" extending lead.
The dog can be arrested at any required distance on the lead. Useful for dogs which are reluctant to come when called.

There are many books which teach you to teach your dog obedience routines, some to a high degree of perfection, but it is all done on the same principle . . . show the dog the response you want, reward the response which the dog makes correctly, ignore or reprimand immediately the wrong response.

Coming when called should always be a pleasure to the dog, you must never call the dog to be punished, it will be too late to associate with the offending action anyway. Coming to the owner should be fun, rewarding or just enjoyable, then you will not have those tussles when a dog refuses to be caught. If you take your dog for exercise off the lead, call it to you when you are *not* just going to put on the lead to go home. Call it for praise and fuss and then let it run free again, so that calling does not end in the non-rewarding action of going on the lead.

Some young dogs will tease, coming to within a foot or so of your hand and then dodging away again. The remedy for these is the Flexi-lead, which can be extended to give the dog a long run, and then reeled in again, or a very long length of rope attached to the collar which you can step on to arrest the dog when it thinks it can evade you.

When playing with sticks or balls which the young dog retrieves, make the dog bring the object right to your hand . . . never chase after it, the dog will always win, and while this may be fun once or twice, it could develop into a "dominating" habit, with you as the under-dog.

The action you are teaching must be properly completed before the dog is rewarded. If you praise when it is half-sitting, half-sitting is all you will ever get.

Formal teaching of this kind is best done for very short periods, several times a day, and not when the dog is anticipating some other treat, like a walk. Just before feeding is an appropriate time for a little drill, the puppy having to "sit" and perhaps not approach the dish until you give the word. Your puppy's full attention will be on you at this time, so the lesson will sink in quickly.

It is a pity if you have to shut your companion dog out when visitors call, or when you cannot take it with you in the car, so try to accustom the dog to all sorts of situations as it grows up. Try to anticipate the problems that may occur and jolly the puppy along at all times. Do not forget the magic bean bag or empty drink tin which helps you administer discipline from a distance. Do not, however, let the puppy play with this object afterwards . . . retrieve it yourself unobtrusively to use another time. You may have to have several bean bags at strategic points about the house.

Playing with dogs is fun and very good for adults too, whose opportunity for foolish playing may be limited. Dogs enjoy hide and seek, hunt the slipper and other games which stretch their mental powers. You will find your dog enjoys solving puzzles . . . you may ask it to go through a door when the way is blocked by boxes, and see how the dog finds its own solution. The agility tests now often featured on television will give you ideas for ladder climbing, tunnel crawling and other agility feats.

Wrestling with big dogs can be fun for the young and fit, but it can be a dangerous pastime in that the dog can always win, and this is a very bad move for dominant or pushy dogs. In general it is better not to play rough games with big and dominant guard dogs, and never to let children do so at all. Never end the game in such a way that the dog feels it has won, always end the game when you say so . . . "That's Enough" or "Finish" can be the word, but say it calmly, not on a note of panic when you are losing the struggle. Reward the puppy when it stops on command. Tug-of-war games are very popular in big breed puppies, they play such games with their litter mates, but it is not a good move to put yourself in competition with the dog when the dog might win. Tugging and snatching can produce vicious tendencies in even quite young puppies.

Careful, thoughtful and consistent management of your dog will pay dividends later on. You should end with a dog which understands its position in the hierarchy and is a pleasure to own. Not only that, you get the reflected glory of knowing that your very agreeable dog, obedient but not cowed, is due to your own efforts. Let this be the best dog you ever owned.

Section IV

YOUR DOG
IN ADOLESCENCE

15

GROWING UP

BITCHES and dogs reach puberty when they are between six and seven months old though in some bitches it may be as early as four months or as late as twenty-two months. There is no clear-cut reason for the difference in onset, but large breeds tend to be later, and possibly a diet low in protein may be a contributory cause.

In the male dog there is no obvious sign that this phase in their life has been reached, except that around this time the dog will perfect his leg-cocking action so that he can territory-mark efficiently . . . his early efforts will have been inaccurate and unsteady, to say the least. At the beginning of puberty, the male hormones tend to be out of control for a time and the dog may be seen trying to mate inanimate objects, or even people. It is imperative to discourage this behaviour firmly and without delay, otherwise it may build up into a major problem. Immediate, effective punishment (the thrown object being particularly useful), is necessary at this time. During this stage it is unwise to leave the dog with children, who may encourage the dog's behaviour because it strikes them as amusing. In most dogs, the hormonal level adjusts spontaneously over a few weeks or months and this behaviour will not be a problem again, provided you do not fall to the temptation of using the dog at stud just once.

As we have said, the male should either be a career stud dog, with a steady supply of bitches coming to him or he should not be used at all. Since, unless your dog is a very big show winner, invitations to use him at stud will be very rare indeed, it is best to disregard this aspect of his life altogether. The very worst thing to do, when the dog is practising adolescent mating behaviour, would be to put him to a bitch at that time, although many owners think this is the solution to their problem.

You would also be most unwise to bring the dog into contact with an in-season, or about to be in-season bitch when this behaviour is occurring.

Young dogs that are just beginning to realise their masculinity may make more determined efforts to escape from your garden; re-double your vigilance, and check on

Fig. 15. **How to reinforce dominance and enhance your status.** As pack leader hold the dog as illustrated as part of the domination routine.

the fencing. Keep the dog well exercised and occupied through this phase and that will make it pass more quickly. A large number of people have dogs which exhibit hypersexual behaviour because they were not properly dominated at this time, but there is no need for you to have one.

The onset of puberty in the bitch is marked by her first heat or season, the period of time when the bitch is attractive to dogs and will allow mating. Bitches are normally stated to come into season twice a year, but the interval varies a great deal in individuals, giving sometimes eight, ten, or twelve months between heats, although a bitch's pattern, once established, is usually much the same throughout life. The form of the bitch's season and the false pregnancy which is likely to follow it has been described in an earlier chapter.

Although bitches are usually rather excitable during

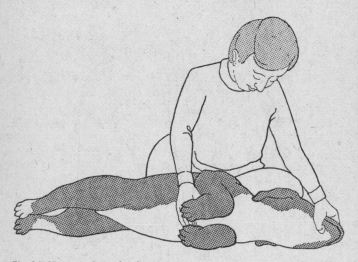

Fig. 16. How to show dominance.
Hold the dog as illustrated to show dominance.

their season, and just before it, there is not any marked change in temperament. Some bitches feel acute distress while undergoing a false pregnancy and they may be possessive or even aggressive in their efforts to guard a litter no-one else can see. Understandable as this is, it is a very bad policy to sympathise with the bitch, because this reinforces the belief that she has puppies to care for. The best ploy is to jolly the bitch out of her broodiness, to give her more exercise and very little opportunity to retire to her bed with "the puppies". If she shows dominant behaviour, exert your dominance by putting her in a submissive position and holding her there. Stand over her and lift her front legs off the ground, make her go through her obedience responses several times and do not show her overmuch affection until she does something to your command. If the bitch becomes shy, retiring and nervous during her false pregnancy and nursing, build her up with plenty of praise and a lot of outdoor activity. Remove the objects she is guarding as substitute puppies discreetly. If you make a big scene about removing them you may lose!

While all this trauma may be avoided by controlling the bitch's heat by surgery or chemical methods, it is generally agreed that this should not be done before the first heat, but the first one is not usually so intense as those to come. Discuss the matter with your veterinary surgeon who will be glad to advise you.

There are a number of other inappropriate behaviours which may appear at this time as the dog reaches maturity. Males, in the large breeds particularly, may exert themselves and become defiant, probably as a bid for pack leadership. Other problem conditions are dealt with in the following pages.

16

PREVENTION OF BAD HABITS

Excessive Barking

Barking is mainly a protest against isolation, or alarm barking at unidentified sounds or movements. In the first case the remedy is obvious, stop isolating the puppy. We have mentioned that some breeds find continuous barking comes very easily to them, and so the owner must not encourage the dog by going to it, even if the intention is to punish the dog. The discomfort of punishment may be less worrying to the dog than isolation, and so barking is reinforced by making visits to punish. Leave the dog for short periods only. To prevent excessive alarm barking, the owner should avoid stimulating the dog by excited commands such as "Who's That?" etc. Alarm barking will almost certainly come naturally when the dog is mature and there is no need to stimulate this behaviour.

Barking at everyday non-threatening noises should be ignored, so that behaviour is extinguished, and the puppy can be positively taught by reward, to bark at exceptional events.

Nervous owners may find it useful to try to control their own "alarm signals" when there is a knock on the door. If you "jump out of your skin" it is understandable that the dog will pick up your fright reaction and make an unwarranted amount of noise. "Stop", "That's Enough" or "Quiet" are useful words to teach to turn off barking which is prolonged, although most dogs manage to have the last word.

Barking while the owner is out can be a problem which grows out of a good thing. We want our dog to reveal its presence, to deter intruders, but we do not want it to go on so long as to annoy the neighbours. There is also the definite probability that a guarding breed, frustrated at not being able to do an effective job in turning the caller away, may destroy something in the room in order to work off its emotions. It may be that keeping the dog in a room where it can see the front door, and know the caller has gone away may lessen the frustration; it may also speed the caller's departure! You may have to use wired glass at the window as an angry guard dog will go through glass without a second thought. Another solution may be a notice (which can be bought at big dog shows or through the dog press), which gives a picture of the relevant breed and has the wording DO NOT KNOCK, I AM IN CHARGE HERE! This can be put into a front window when you are going to be out . . . it should not encourage burglars. The police say that a dog in the house is the biggest deterrent for the opportunist sneak thief, and the vast majority of burglaries are of this nature. The problem should not arise if you do not encourage over-barking in the first instance.

Stealing

As dogs do not have any moral sense, it is incorrect to speak of stealing in connection with a dog helping itself to food left around within reach. You can teach your dog not to touch its own meal until given permission, and you can also, by means of NO, stop the dog from approaching a box of sweets open on a coffee table, but remember the temptation is great if you are not in attendance.

Do not feed your puppy titbits from the table or, in fact, titbits at all unless it has performed some command. This is a counsel of perfection and if you have already established the habit of the dog begging and becoming ever more pushing while you are eating, *ignore* the dog, and insist that everyone else does so also. It may take a number of weeks, but if no human ever back-slides by giving the dog anything from the table, the behaviour will in the end be extinguished. On the other hand, how would any of us have got through our childhood without the dog at hand to dispose of those horrid bits of gristle which made so much trouble at meals? Where there are tiny children, prone to drop crumbs and crusts, it is very difficult to persuade the dog that it is not a good thing to sit close. You can order the dog into its bed in the same room until the meal is over, when it can have a reward for waiting patiently.

Excessive Biting

Excessive biting at the hands or ankles of humans usually responds to the standard methods of scolding or mild punishment at the time of the crime. These means should be tried in the first instance coupled by strong dominance procedures by the person concerned. If there is any sign that this treatment is aggravating rather than solving the problem, as it may just possibly do in a very dominant dog, the person being "attacked" should stay quite still, not withdrawing hand or ankle. At the same time, or even before the "attack", some stimulus that distracts the dog's attention should be applied.

Excessive Chewing

Puppies chew things as a way of exploring their environment and also to break down barriers between them and the place they want to be. The puppy chews as a natural behaviour, and when the second teeth are coming through, at about 4–6 months of age, the need to ease the mouth by chewing is quite evident. Puppies should be given one or two chewable objects, a log stripped of bark, a large marrow bone, or rawhide chews, and when a puppy is discovered at work on something else, the chew object should be substituted and the dog distracted on to its own object. Dogs which chew their own coats, or their paws are desperately bored and frustrated and the remedy is obvious.

Dogs which tend to chew doors when left alone may be cured by magic punishments, if you can come back to administer them when the dog thinks you have gone, or it is possible to buy sprays (via the dog press), which deter them from chewing a specific area.

Submissive Urination

Until now we have principally discussed the need for the owner to become dominant over the pet, but in the case of the shy or nervous puppy excessive domination can lead to submissive urination, the kind of puppy that fills your shoes as you say hello to it. If you get the submissive urination response you will know that you have pushed punishment to its limit, or that you have a puppy that is right at the bottom of the domination chain so that it feels that it must make obeisance to everyone it encounters.

You must make immediate moves to restore or build up the dog's confidence. All corrective procedures involving punishments of any kind should be stopped and the puppy should be praised and rewarded for all correct behaviour *and* for not showing inappropriate behaviour such as submissive urination.

Remember that a submissive dog of this kind should be "jollied" rather than sympathised. Bend down to greet the puppy rather than patting it from above and let the dog take the initiative in greeting callers, but stop these tactics when you have reached a good level of confidence in the dog; do not let it go too far and into dominance.

Behaviour Induced by Other People

However well you and your family co-operate in managing the dog, you may find that bad behaviour patterns are being instilled and rewarded by people outside your control. It is not uncommon to find that neighbours are giving their scrap food to your dog through the fence. They will later on be very surprised and annoyed when the dog is barking there for attention and a free meal.

Similarly your dog may become over-excited and frustrated by children dragging sticks along the railings as they pass. You may be angry with the dog for damaging your flowers, but the impetus to do so was almost forced upon a dog protecting its territory. It is better to risk achieving a "coldness" between neighbours by asking them not to attract or talk to your dog in any way unless you are with it, rather than have your good management ruined by people who do not have to bear the consequences.

It is not unknown for workmen, dustmen and so on to tease the dog unmercifully while it is young and then to complain of its aggressive tendencies later on. Supervision of the dog at all times is the best preventative.

Section V

YOUR DOG IN ADULTHOOD

17

ADULT DOG

ALTHOUGH the management of your puppy has proceeded well, there is always the natural tendency for the dog to develop new behaviour patterns which may be undesirable in your pack. You must be prepared to notice what is happening and to be ready to extinguish the behaviour before it becomes an ingrained habit. The following sections will also be of great help to those people who already have less than perfect pets, because the dog was obtained when adult or because the early training their dog received lacked purpose.

While studies made by animal behaviourists, particularly in America, have made it possible to establish a number of basic principles which can be used to correct inappropriate behaviour in dogs, it can be difficult to know the remedy to use in any one case. Every problem is different, the nature and physical capabilities of dog owners are different, the homes are different and the places and circumstances in which the inappropriate behaviours occur are different. Sometimes individual prescriptions for management are needed, and if, after following the basic advice given in this book, you feel that the problem behaviour is getting worse, or it is beyond you to dominate the dog, then we strongly advise you to seek professional help. Your veterinary surgeon may be able to help or put you in touch with a specialist in animal behaviour.

Because the results of an attack by a vicious, uncontrolled dog, even quite a small-sized dog can be so disastrous, especially when children are involved, we strongly advise that you seek professional advice early where biting and attacking are the problem.

A behaviour problem that a dog has learned or acquired can be cured or at least reduced by five methods:

Extinction, Counter-conditioning, Systematic Desensitisation, Punishment and Flooding.

Extinction

This simply means that the frequency of a behaviour will reduce if the behaviour no longer "pays off" to the dog's benefit. If titbits are not given at the table the dog will eventually stop expecting them. But, conversely, the dog that has been trained to sit on command will lose that ability if it is ignored when it responds.

Dogs can feel rewarded when we do not intend them to, and many owners are unaware that they are reinforcing the very behaviour which they would like to stop. The small dog which rushes to the front door, barking excitedly when the doorbell rings will have this behaviour reinforced if the owner strokes the dog, talks to it in what is believed to be a calming way, perhaps even picks it up into her arms before opening the door. All this is a rewarding procedure which will certainly register as "paying off" to the dog, and it will be repeated at every opportunity. If this owner was aiming to teach the dog to bark wildly when the doorbell rang she could hardly do better! The dog will continue to lay on this hysterical scene in order to get its owner's attention. The appropriate corrective behaviour would be to shut the dog away and ignore it, or teach it some more acceptable form of greeting.

Another reinforcing behaviour often made inadvertently is an attempt to comfort a dog during thunderstorms. The dog is cuddled and fussed while it shivers and shakes, and the owner is conveying as strongly as possible to the dog that it is right to be afraid of storms because it gets its reward in special attention. In fact, excessive fear of thunderstorms is unnatural in the dog, and it is almost always generated by the owner who wants or needs a transference object for their own fear. It is noticeable that dogs which live in the flight path of airports do not fear the noise of thunder, jet planes or fireworks, as noise is one of the everyday environmental happenings. This emphasises the need to acclimatise puppies to noise. Dogs are very easily conditioned to take up our own phobias. They watch their owners constantly and pick up our moods far more quickly than we realise. Especially where there is great devotion between dog and owner, a transference of fear is quickly made. If both dog and owner can jolly each other along, instead of sympathising, if they play a game, or put on some music, owner and dog can help each other out of a fear.

An even more bizarre conditioning happened in the case of an owner who had, since childhood a great fear of small wild birds coming into the house. She was prepared to tolerate this failing in herself, but she noticed that her very large and stalwart guard dog was cowering under the table, shivering and casting horrified glances at a very cheerful little sparrow perched on the draining board. The owner realised that she had "told" the dog, by her own behaviour, that the correct response to little birds was extreme fear, and the dog was showing this behaviour although a fear of birds is quite unnatural to dogs. Fortunately, the sight of so large and fierce a dog showing extreme submission to a sparrow served to point out to the owner how ridiculous and unfounded her own behaviour was. The need to bolster up the dog's confidence helped the owner correct what had been a longstanding phobia.

If your dog has an inappropriate learned behaviour, think around the subject and see if you can identify how the behaviour or the measures you take to correct it are rewarding to the dog. Consider that you may be generating the behaviour yourself. Remember, being comforted, given attention, or even mild punishment can be rewarding to the dog. Being ignored is never rewarding.

Counter-conditioning

By this we mean training the dog to acquire a new behaviour, or to make a different response to a stimulus in place of the inappropriate behaviour. To return to the dog which barks hysterically at the door bell, this animal could be trained to find it more profitable, in that it would get better rewards, if it sat quietly in its basket when the bell rang. Instead of just ignoring the dog, which the owner may find hard to do, a positive training system is started, using the modern learning and teaching techniques. To recapitulate, these are:

1. Reward the dog very quickly for a correct response.
2. Give verbal praise, but as the desire to respond is enhanced by the *value* of the reward, it is helpful to accompany praise and petting by a food reward.
3. The dog learns most quickly if the reward is forthcoming every time it responds correctly.
4. The dog retains the behaviour pattern longer (it becomes a habit), if, after the dog is responding correctly every time, rewards are given only sometimes.
5. The dog will lose a behaviour pattern entirely if that behaviour is never rewarded.

Systematic Desensitisation

This is a specialised technique, generally not suitable for owner application as it requires in most cases co-operation from other people. It is used to break down anxiety or fear by exposing the dog to a very low level of that fear, rewarding the dog when it can tolerate that level and gradually increasing the stimulus until the full strength fear can be faced and tolerated.

A dog's fears are usually based upon lack of early conditioning to some factor, for example, car riding or the company of men, or an early bad experience, perhaps unavoidable pain at the vet's or a very strong punishment by a previous owner.

We rescued a dog which had a bold, even aggressive, temperament except for just one thing, she was terrified into a jelly by the sight or even the smell of a *feather*. We deduced that in her early life she had torn up a feather cushion and received drastic punishment. She was not, however, cured of destruction, just afraid of cushions or even a stray feather on the ground.

We began counter-conditioning by putting just one feather within a yard of her food bowl. With reluctance, she would eventually walk in a wide circle all round the feather to reach her bowl, and she was praised for doing so. Gradually the feather was put nearer the bowl on successive days, and every time she endured its closeness, she was rewarded. If the fear persisted, the feather was not removed and the dog was ignored, but no other punishments or frighteners were allowed to spoil her day. She got no evident sympathy or petting which would have reinforced the fear. After quite a long time the counter-conditioning has worked to the extent that the bitch can sit on a feather cushion, but she will still avoid a stray feather lying in the grass. This behaviour is ignored.

Unreasonable fear of the veterinary surgery needs to be eliminated as a really frightened dog can set back its treatment and outlook for recovery. Desensitisation will need a positive approach and will make great demands on your time, but in this case, it will be well worth while. Begin by sitting in the waiting room with the dog for just a few minutes, at a time when there is no need to see the vet. Reward the dog when it can sit without fear, ignore it when it fails, and gradually increase the length of time you spend in the waiting room. Later on, the nurses and receptionists will be only too glad to take part by "examining" the dog gently. Give each stage plenty of time and do not proceed to the next "ordeal" until the previous one is tolerated with complete unconcern, and anticipation of the delicious reward. Lifting the dog on to the examination table is a big progression, but if you go when the main surgery is over, the vet will be quite happy to co-operate in breaking down the dog's fear. The secret is to take desensitisation in very tiny steps, not going beyond what the dog can tolerate. Too big a step forward will ruin all the work you have put in, and you will have to begin at the beginning again. Everyone feels admiration for an owner who is taking a lot of trouble to cure a dog's behaviour problem in a constructive way, rather than following the too easy path of getting rid of the dog, so you should find everyone at the surgery only too willing to help you.

It may be that, having got your dog completely free of surgery fear, you do not need to visit there again for some time, and so there is no opportunity to continue to reward the dog for this aspect of good behaviour. It may thus be useful to repeat the last few steps in the desensitisation programme at intervals.

Punishment

Punishment can be effectively used to stop an undesirable behaviour, if the following points are recognised:

1. Punishment may be either the administration of a painful stimulus (painful ranging from "surprising" to shaming to physical pain) . . . or the withdrawal of a pleasurable experience. If a child is naughty, you may say, "now you will have no sweets today", or "you will not watch your favourite TV programme". But deprivations in the future, even within an hour, mean nothing to the dog. The deprivation must happen at once and the most forceful one is withdrawing your attention, both in speech, actions and glances.

2. Punishment to be effective must be administered immediately, hence the use of the thrown object and magic.

3. Punishment must be strong enough to disrupt the inappropriate behaviour.

4. Punishment must not be so strong that it causes prolonged suffering and misery to the dog.

5. Punishment is often not effective on its own. Ideally the dog should be counter-conditioned to perform another acceptable behaviour, so giving the dog a chance to "escape" into a behaviour which will bring it praise and a reward.

6. Shy and nervous dogs should not be punished.

7. Punishment must be used with great caution during the sensitive period, 7–14 weeks in young puppies.

8. Punishment that involves hitting or slapping an animal may be counter-productive as the dog may fight back or take it as an invitation to play, i.e. a reward. It is extremely difficult to inflict adequate physical punishment on a strong dog in the larger breeds without entering the realms of brutality.

Social isolation is generally more effective, except that

it can be difficult to apply immediately, but a sensitive dog can feel a change in atmosphere between its owner and itself. If your dog commits a major disobedience while on a walk, for instance, you can put it on the lead, and "turn off" immediately the pleasing sounds you make, put it in the car in silence, do not speak to the dog on the way home etc. The dog well adjusted to its owner will notice the difference. Talking to the dog . . . saying, "you were a bad dog, weren't you" *is rewarding with attention,* don't do it!

Flooding, or response prevention as it is sometimes called, is a technique that is sometimes used to overcome phobias or major bad habits such as chicken or sheep chasing. Essentially the idea is to expose the animal to a fear inducing stimulus but in a situation in which the animal cannot escape from the fear object.

This technique works in some humans, for instance, the owner previously mentioned who was afraid of small birds might be treated by being shut in an aviary, having been previously conditioned by being shown pictures of birds, and then touching stuffed birds. It takes a lot of courage for a phobic human to submit to flooding technique and there is a great deal of doubt whether it can ever be effective in the dog which cannot be prepared in the same way, and the phobia may be intensified by this treatment.

Flooding was tried on Anna, the Doberman, when she developed a phobia about being in a room in which a log fire was burning. Probably Anna had been burnt by a spark from such a fire, so her reluctance to approach was understandable. Attempts were made to force her to stay close to a log fire, but although she was not made more fearful, she became very agitated. Anna could not be made to enjoy a log fire and she would still go out of the room if she could. The problem was solved by counter-conditioning, by giving a food reward for sitting or lying quietly by a small coal fire, then a larger coal fire, then adding one log, and later making larger fires until Anna takes no notice of a roaring, spitting fire. Now that unreasonable avoidance of fires has been overcome, Anna is free to take evasive action when the sparks fly for, undoubtedly, dogs are at some risk on the hearthrug, and Anna knew it.

Sheep-chasing and chicken-killing are major crimes in pet dogs. Although the owners should always be covered by third-party insurance to cover the very great financial loss which may accrue to the farmer, it is a behaviour which must be eradicated immediately if the dog is to go on living. The method used was to tie a dead chicken, or part of a dead lamb or other animal which was chased to the dog's collar so that it must live with its "shame" for a number of hours or days. It may have been that the rescued dog which was so afraid of feathers, as mentioned earlier, had been given this ordeal. She would certainly have never willingly approached a feathered creature or object again.

Another method is aversion therapy, having first made the dog feel nauseous, but this needs specialised supervision.

Flooding is a powerful curative technique only to be used with great care. All behaviour problems in dogs need an individual approach. It is necessary to look closely at what is happening, to try to recall when the particular behaviour started and after that to select the method or combination of methods best suited to the cure.

18

CURING PROBLEM BEHAVIOUR

INAPPROPRIATE behaviours in dogs fall into five main categories: Aggressive, destructive, disobedient, introverted (that is, phobias), and sexual.

Aggressive Behaviour

There are several types of aggression and the cause may be different in each case, so it is important to establish the cause of the problem. Is the aggression the result of fear, pain, a reaction to over-dominance or associated with sex drive (hyper-sexuality)? The corrective measures employed will vary greatly and what may be effective in one case will not necessarily work in another.

Because it would be so easy to make an aggressive dog even more fierce by the wrong correction, it is advisable to seek your veterinary surgeon's advice and help before beginning any remedial action. Your understanding of the behaviour modification principles described in this book will help you both to identify the cause of the problem and interpret correctly the advice given.

A *fear-biter* is a very dangerous dog indeed. This is the basically nervous dog which uses its teeth because it is unsure of its position in the pack and in its world. Unfortunately, many rescued dogs turn out to be fear-biters because of incidents in their past which new owners cannot be aware of. Desensitisation and counter-conditioning are the methods most usually used; punishment must be avoided because this type of dog cannot take punishment. Very severe physical punishment may stop the dog attacking the person who punishes but may make the dog resentful and even more fierce with other people.

Pain-induced Aggression

It is a natural reaction to pain to show aggression and any dog injured, for instance in a road accident, may bite the person who comes to help it. Some dogs which have had the experience of pain may become aggressive when they think they are about to be hurt. The best way to avoid such aggression is to take great care not to make the dog fearful. Some ear infections are extremely painful for some time even after veterinary treatment; it is only reasonable not to touch the dog at the head end at this time and to *warn everyone* else, especially children, that the dog is intensely sensitive in the ear region at this time. Grooming routines must be adjusted to tender areas and the dog should be liberally rewarded when it allows you to attend to a wound without protest. Punishment should never be used where pain is the basis for aggression.

It may be that you have not noticed a painful area on the dog so this is something which should be investigated when a normally even-tempered dog acts in an aggressive manner.

Learnt Aggression

Dogs can be taught to be aggressive but this is very seldom necessary in the traditional guarding breeds. Owners sometimes worry that the dog they bought as a guard seems to be everyone's best friend, but many of the guard breeds are slow to mature. They remain puppies up to two years old or even longer, and their guarding ability may never be overtly demonstrated, if the need does not occur, but unless you bought from very degenerate stock, the guard instinct will rise to the surface when needed. Some guard dogs need to feel affection for their owners and their home territory before they will guard; being ignored and not treated as part of the family pack can nullify the instinct to protect.

Guard instinct should not be encouraged and reinforced in large breed dogs which the owner will not be able to control should the aggressive tendencies become exaggerated; children should be especially warned not to encourage fierceness or aggression towards people or other dogs, even as a game. The situation could so easily get out of hand with disastrous consequences.

The more usual situation happens with the smaller breed dog, in the example visualised earlier, when the dog rushes towards the front door barking. Similarly, owners will often unwittingly train their pet to fight by being nervous that it may do so. On the approach of another dog, often quite a civil dog but one of a big breed, the owner begins to restrain and calm his dog, and may even pick the dog up . . . "to prevent a fight". They are, without knowing it, teaching their dog to be wary of other canines. Many dog fights would never occur if only the owners could have faith that the dogs will sort out their rank and role for themselves, if left to proceed without human interference. Very dominant dogs should not be exercised in public places unless under strict control, and if they must be so exercised, they ideally should wear a muzzle, both as a warning to other owners and to prevent them biting. A dog knows when it is handicapped and will not pick a fight when muzzled.

Sometimes dogs can become over-excited in a game and will attempt to chase children playing on bicycles . . . the dog is rewarded because the child pedals faster and the bicycle goes away. The best remedial behaviour is to "set up" a cycling scene and then use the thrown object to deter the dog from following the cyclist.

Jealousy Between Dogs

Where there is more than one dog in a household, and especially where they are of the same sex and roughly the same age, it is not uncommon to find that aggressive feelings will lead to fights between the dogs. In this situation there is not usually any aggression towards the human members of the pack although in breaking up a fight, people do get bitten by mistake although even the fiercest fighter will desist when it feels its teeth go into human flesh, if that was not its target.

The situation can often be cured by the owner enhancing his domination over both dogs by instigating regular training periods and making a point of holding the dogs in submissive postures. Dominance should also be shown when the low growling begins which signals the start of a fight. Obviously it makes sense not to allow any "property" to be owned by either dog, all beds etc. being communal. If one toy generates possessive feelings, it makes sense to remove it entirely, and to feed the dogs separately.

In some cases it may help if the owner reinforces the position of the most dominant dog, giving it privileges above the other, which should, in theory, be happy to have its submissive role defined for it. It may not sound fair to "kick" the underdog and praise the dominant one, but in some cases the underdog is more contented and comfortable when it accepts its role in life. It may equally be true that the under-dog will continue to make bids for dominance and the rivalry will simmer away for many years. Where one of these smouldering feuds exists, the dogs often take the opportunity to break into a fight when there is another excitement . . . visitors being welcomed is the classic one. If you know this is likely to happen, take the dominant dog with you to open the door, let it be greeted first, and then put away while the other comes out to be introduced. Two Boxer bitches fighting in the middle of the room are apt to wreck the best of cocktail parties! Surprisingly, the two participants in a long-standing war may be the best of friends for most of the time and the jealousy fights do not result in very grievous wounds, probably being more roaring than biting.

If a fight does break out, within the home or between unfamiliar dogs outside, it is important to know how to break it up with the least damage to people or dogs. Small dogs sometimes deliberately aggravate large ones, and the big dog's natural behaviour is to put the smaller down into submissive position. If only the owners can be persuaded not to scream, panic, or interfere, the smaller dog will eventually be allowed to get up and will walk away unscathed. It will be noticed that the "victim" knows its own role quite well, and it will submit quietly; it is when people try to pull the aggressor away that the messages get all mixed up and injuries may be inflicted.

An evenly-matched fight is almost impossible to break up by physical means and people should be restrained from playing the hero and plunging in to try to open the jaws of one dog to make it free another. Subtle surprise acts best . . . a hose of water directed on the pair, even a car horn sounded loudly, the doorbell rung if in a house, all serve to distract the fighters, if only momentarily. The trick is to be ready to separate the two effectively at once otherwise your ruse will have been useless and the pair will be gripping each other again. If one dog is still on a lead, do resist the temptation to pull it up on its hind legs, revealing its soft under-belly to be bitten. Dogs normally take fight wounds on the neck and front legs and these are far less damaging than to the abdominal area or male sexual organs.

Fights in the kitchen, over a dropped crumb, can be broken up by banging a saucepan on the sink, any loud noise serves as a distraction so that one of the participants can be thrown outside. If the dogs are wearing collars, they can be induced to loosen their grip by the collar being twisted, momentarily to choking point.

Jumping Up

Jumping up is probably the single most annoying behaviour which a dog can perform and yet, when it is done as an expression of pleasure and greeting it becomes very hard to curb. Essentially, jumping up is a dominant greeting, the exact opposite of the submissive action of rolling over and spontaneously urinating in your shoe. Jumping up may be cured by increasing the owner's dominant role, by stopping the reinforcement of the behaviour by allowing it to lead to a pleasurable experience for the dog, by diverting the dog's attention (counter-conditioning), by immediate punishment and by very firm pushing down. It is important to make sure that pushing down does not escalate into a rewarding play situation in which the dog wins. All games that involve hyper-activity and rough play should be stopped, since they encourage jumping up.

It is pleasant to be greeted enthusiastically by your dog, but you will not want your best clothes ruined, nor will you want battering by eager paws when you are tired after work. Friends may not be so dog-orientated as you are and the action that you know to be an enthusiastic greeting may look to them very like an attack. If they react with fear, the dog is encouraged to take more aggressive action and what began as an expression of joy may end in an ugly situation. In summary the actions to take are:

1. First, teach your dog to sit and stay, using the learning principles as before, rewarding the dog with a morsel of food when it obeys . . . some people come home armed with a canteen biscuit just for this purpose.

2. Then be prepared to ignore any over-exuberant greeting, at the same time saying NO, or DON'T Jump Up (not down, which means another action).

3. Do not reward jumping up with praise, petting, pushing or kicking, which may be interpreted as a game.

4. As soon as the dog is calmer, tell it to sit and stay,

reward obedience to this command promptly with food, not petting.

5. Once the dog has learnt to sit in such situations you can then walk towards it and bending down slightly, stroke and pet the animal at the same time applying a downward pressure on the back over the shoulders.

6. An over-active dog may be distracted by giving it a glove or a purse to carry off to release its tensions . . . some people carry a special object with them for the purpose. It is not usually damaged, just carried about and may be tactfully retrieved later for use tomorrow.

It would be better if the jumping behaviour never started; it has been found helpful to greet the dog first from the car, opening the door while remaining seated to take the first flush of joy at reunion while reasonably protected. Only after the dog has quietened a little do the passengers get out.

Over-enthusiastic greeting is not a behaviour that can be extinguished easily or quickly, so it is better if you never let it occur. If from puppy days you greet your dog in a crouching position and put it through a domination routine if it shows signs of jumping up, you need not be put in the awkward position of having to train your dog out of being pleased to see you.

Destructive Behaviour

In some cases the natural instinct of the dog to investigate its surroundings with its mouth, which the dog uses much in the way we use our hands, is carried to extremes so that the dog will wreck the house or car when it is left in these places. As we have seen in the chapter on adolescent behaviours, destruction can be caused by frustration, and the need to work off emotional tension as well as when the dog is anxious, angry or bored, and sometimes from sheer mischievousness. Not all dogs are destroyers and it is not easy to see why some are and some not. The most commonly held theory is that some dogs are more mouth-orientated than others. The corrective procedures can be summarised:

1. Give the puppy only a few objects to chew, praise him

occasionally when he chews them. A large non-splintery bone, or a log, perhaps a nylon bone serve, to work off the desire to chew.

2. Never leave the puppy unattended in "good" rooms, remove temptation, or if that is not possible consider the use of a cage or playpen to enclose the dog.

3. Avoid excessive attention to the dog's mouth . . . in some breeds people who mean to exhibit will be very keen to know if the bite is forming in a correct way but resist the temptation to examine the mouth very frequently . . . you can do nothing to help the formation of the bite anyway. Do not play tug-of-war games.

4. Do not isolate the dog as a method of punishment during the sensitive period of puppyhood.

5. Be dominant, make sure you are the pack leader.

6. Before you leave your dog alone, give it physical exercise, and, as often as you can, give it mental problems to solve as well.

7. Accustom the dog to being left gradually, for short times at first and gradually lengthening the time you are away. Always reward generously if the dog has been good. Start when the puppy is young by saying "We won't be long".

8. Leave the light and the radio on, as you would if you were going into another room. This gives the dog the cue that you will be returning shortly. Leave some safe form of heating, so that the dog is warm and relaxed.

9. Do not punish on your return, even if the dog has destroyed something, it is by then too late and may make the problem worse.

10. Most importantly, get into the habit of tidying up before you go out, making sure that only the dog's own toys are available for chewing. Remember, it is your fault if something precious is available.

11. If you have to be away for several hours in the morning, consider picking up the post and newspapers on your way out, so that the numbers of callers to the house are cut down. Frustration is often the reason why a dog attacks doors and window sills.

If your dog is already a destroyer, you will have to use your ingenuity to circumvent the behaviour, as there is no one patent remedy. To be successful you must be prepared to progress slowly, and make sure the dog never succeeds in destroying things . . . this will be a win for him. It may take a lot of time and patience, but it will probably pay you to make a false departure and then come back very quickly to see what the dog is doing. Perhaps you can go into the garden to work, pretending to be out, and then you may get a clue to the trigger factor . . . does the dog start to destroy immediately the door closes on you, or only after a caller at the front door . . . only after you have been gone an hour or two?

If you are able to rig up a booby trap which will give the dog a big fright when he attacks a cupboard, or if your patience lasts so long that you can apply that loaded water pistol through the keyhole, you will have won a big battle, saved yourself pounds of damaged woodwork, and improved your companion dog no end.

There are deterrent aerosol sprays available which not only put a nasty taste on woodwork but if you take the dog to the chewed object and spray it in his presence, the hissing of the spray, and probably the fine fall-out droplets, are distasteful too.

When you go out, give the dog a cue that you will not be long by leaving the radio playing . . . and do not make a performance of saying goodbye . . . simply say "Look after the house" . . . it is the hello when you come back which should be joyous, with reward if the dog has got through without tooth-marking anything.

Disobedience and Unruliness

There is a popular belief that dogs are not ready for training until they are six months old, probably generated by the many formal obedience training groups which have their eye on competitive work. It is a pity that this myth has become so strong, for many of the more energetic breeds are, by the time they are six months old, past the point of no return for early conditioning. It cannot be said too often that management, that is, training, of the puppy starts at the moment it becomes yours, and by the time the puppy is six months old it should be doing what you want it to do nearly all the time. A period of rebellion may set in during adolescence, but this is easier to cure when you have the basic foundations to build upon.

As with children, and in so many ways young dogs are like young children, inconsistency of teaching also produces disobedience. The improper use of punishment, especially calling the dog in to be punished, produces a dog which will not come at all for fear of what may happen to it. Punishment which the dog does not connect with the deed produces bewilderment, resentment, or plain non-co-operation in the dog.

It is quite easy to go to the other extreme and command the dog so much that it has no freedom of action at all. Some dogs will be submissive and afraid to move without direction, others may be rebels and delight in any opportunity to run off and defy their owner to catch up with them. The whole key to good dog management is to let life remain fun for the dog; let the good things happen and prevent, by your vigilance, the dog doing wrong.

Dogs and their owners train very hard, several nights each week sometimes, for the competitive obedience trials which culminate in top competition at shows. At these classes the dogs learn a set of formalised movements which are far removed from the things we want our dogs to do in normal life. If you wish to make obedience competition your hobby, by all means join a class with your dog, but keep up the management which you began as a puppy, it will in any case prove a good foundation for competitive work.

Lead Training

Large dogs which pull on the lead are tiring to take out and a nuisance to themselves and others. It is essential to train the dog to the lead when you are *not going anywhere* . . . on a separate occasion from an exercise trip. Choose a quiet stretch of road, and be ready to reverse direction every time the dog pulls ahead. Dog then finds itself behind you, and if you swing a rolled newspaper or stick in front of the nose the dog will be deterred from forging ahead. Keep the lead short, with the object of the dog being just at your side . . . "heel" is not a very companionable position for a pet dog. Your patience and staying power is what counts; reverse and reverse and reverse until the dog has got it right. Do fifty yards with the dog in the right position and then praise, reward and break off for the day. Repeat tomorrow and the next day until walking by your side is the dog's natural position. It can help to take a "pulling" dog out with another one which has perfect manners in this respect.

You may want to use the word "Back" when the dog is pulling ahead, giving a significant jerk to show what you mean. Choke or check chains, when put on and used properly, give maximum control over a strong dog while it is being trained. The use of body harness is to be deplored, as these are an incentive to pulling and will also cause a distorted movement of the front legs.

Pulling and bad behaviour on the lead can be cured.

1. Work at lead training when you have no objective in view except perfecting the dog's behaviour.
2. Do not try to train when the dog is going for its walk.
3. Persevere, and reward!

Car Sickness

Car sickness can be genuine motion sickness, in which case it will be necessary to seek a veterinary surgeon's advice and suitable medication. Beware of using preparations intended for human car and air sickness on the dog, even in children's dose . . . the canine reaction to these medicines can be quite unpredictable and frightening. If you are carrying your dog in the back of an estate car, you may find it a salutary experience to try a short ride as a passenger in the dog's position . . . there can be a great deal of vibration in the luggage space, enough to cause discomfort to the dog. Some dogs ride more comfortably on the floor of the car where they cannot see out.

It may be that car sickness is the expression of a phobia arising from a bad experience. Tigger very much enjoyed car rides until he had the misfortune to be thrown from a car which was in a minor crash. Tigger ran off across country and by the time the drivers had sorted themselves out he was nowhere to be seen. This dog, a very well adjusted companion animal, obedient and properly dominated by his owner, for the first time in his life refused to come when called. Although he did not travel far from the crash site, he took shelter in woodland nearby and deliberately avoided all attempts to recapture him. After twelve hours of fruitless calling and searching, Tigger's owner sat down in a neighbouring field and just waited quietly, knowing that he was in full view of the dog which was hovering in the shelter of trees. Eventually, after a long wait, Tigger very tentatively made his way to his owner, who wisely made no move to catch the dog but spoke gently and encouragingly all the while. This anecdote is told to show how quickly a long-term trust can be shattered by a traumatic incident. We cannot know how the car crash affected the dog; it may have seemed that his owner "threw" him from the car as a punishment. It so happened that Tigger had guilt feelings at the time of the crash, as he normally travelled in the back seat, but had ventured into the front, knowing it was against the rules. His owner had decided to ignore the behaviour "just this once" as they were nearly at their journey's end.

Although it is wrong to assume too much human-type thought in a dog, it seems quite likely that Tigger felt the car crash was a punishment directed at him, and in that case it was decidedly an over-punishment. The story also points to a moral of never allowing a dog to do what you know to be unsafe or wrong, even for a few minutes.

Tigger was unhurt after the crash and not exactly frightened, but better described as disorientated, as if his whole world had crashed about him. If in fact he had regarded the crash as a punishment, this might well have been so.

To continue with his story, he was soon riding again in a hired car quite happily, and we congratulated ourselves that he had not developed a car phobia. This happy idea was shattered when the crashed car was returned to us, Tigger absolutely refused to get into it, and although he was dominated and made to ride in it, and in a successive model of exactly the same type, he never enjoyed car riding and had to be made to accompany us every time. Eventually, we got a car of different make and shape; Tigger got in willingly and is now a very keen motoring dog again, so if your dog has a car phobia, it may be with good reason, and a change of car could help.

The carsick puppy should be taken out for short rides as often as possible, logically, before meals instead of just after. If the puppy drools or vomits, no comment should be made, certainly no sympathy given. In the end puppies, like children, outgrow car sickness if it is virtually ignored, but giving attention, even by turning round constantly to see how the dog is faring, are an encouragement to the dog to vomit, as this species does easily. Make the car ride short but enjoyable by going to a place where the dog can have a walk, not only a trip to the vet or the poodle parlour or to wait in the car while you are shopping.

If you acquire an adult dog which has never had experience of cars, allow it to sit in the car while it is stationary, then to be in the car while it is backed in and out of the garage and so gradually lengthen the drive, but be *jolly* about it, not anxious and sympathetic to the dog. If you have your dog in the garage with you, take care that there are no pools of antifreeze about, this substance is sweet-tasting and very attractive to dogs, but it is a deadly poison.

When the dog first goes out in the car, have someone hold the dog steady if it is a lightweight, being jolted about is unpleasant for humans and dogs. Yorkshire Terriers as a breed tend to be poor travellers and they are best carried in a crate, obtainable in wood or plastic and very useful in many ways for tiny dogs.

If the dog persists in car sickness and there is a long journey to be undertaken, seek advice from your veterinary surgeon about suitable medication.

Shyness

A shy dog is often one that lacked proper socialisation during the sensitive stage of puppyhood, probably through not meeting a sufficient range of people. A dog may also become shy as a result of too hard punishment not correctly administered in relation to the dog's behaviour. Punishment which the dog cannot understand can provoke a fear reaction which may take the form of aggression, or extreme submission, expressed by involuntary urination and evacuation.

If this should happen you have direct evidence that your management is wrong and too harsh for the particular dog you have. All punishment should be stopped and the dog's confidence built up by everyone in its world. The dog should be played with frequently and the dog should be shown the value of interaction with people . . . being friendly should "pay off".

Some dogs are almost permanently "shy" with visitors but are composed and happy with members of the family pack. If it is desired to extend the dog's range of accepted humans, the newcomers should avoid talking to or even looking at the dog. Eventually, after hours, days or even weeks the dog's natural curiosity will allow it to approach, and a food reward should be forthcoming instantly. Visitors should be asked not to call or otherwise to try to attract the shy dog, let it come of its own accord. It can help if a newcomer takes the dog for an enjoyable walk, making this a socialisation period but not, of course, letting the dog off the lead.

The Boisterous Dog

The dog that is too boisterous, too anxious to welcome visitors can be a great source of annoyance and even embarrassment. The temptation is to shut the dog away but that does not solve the problem for punishment by isolation may make the dog hostile to callers or it may lead to room destruction through frustration. It is not easy to put the dog through a domination routine when people are entering the house and claiming your attention, and it is not easy to get visitors to behave as one would wish, neither fearing the dog or exciting it.

One of the best solutions is to shut the dog away until the visitors are welcomed and *seated*, and then to allow the dog to come in, asking visitors not to call it or even concentrate their attention on the dog. The dog will want to investigate the callers and there seems no way around this; any lively dog will want to get the scent of visitors to its pack. The dog should be controlled by the owner so that its approach is as calm as possible, and after a few minutes the dog can be commanded to go to its bed and it should be re-ordered back to its bed if it makes itself a nuisance. Visitors must be asked not to fend the dog off (that is, initiate a play routine), or to give it lumps of sugar or biscuits "to go away". We know that the reverse action will result.

One word of warning about leaving mature guard dogs with visitors to the house (e.g. babysitters). Although extremely pleasant when the owner is at hand, these dogs will drop into a different rôle when left in a room alone with a visitor. The dog, apparently so relaxed and sleeping, may emit low warning growls if the visitor moves' about the room, picks up magazines and books etc. . . . the dog is putting its guarding into effect as well as it knows how. The dog should not be reprimanded . . . in fact, the owner may not know that this behaviour takes place unless the visitor complains, and few do . . . but care should be taken to remove the dog while the owner is away from the room, unless it is suspected that the visitor needs watching.

Guard dogs can also be resentful of visitors walking about the house or garden, although friendly to them while they are sitting in one place. Owner domination and care that the dog does not have the opportunity to harass visitors will save this from becoming a problem. Especial care should be taken of child visitors whose shrill voices and running movements may be outside the experience of a guard dog normally accustomed only to adults.

Licking

Excessive licking of human hands is a sign of submission, often demonstrated by a dog which has been punished for dominating behaviour as a signal for re-admission into good status within the family pack. "Don't Lick" is a command which can be used, while removing hand or face from licking range. Puppies lick their dam's mouth as a signal for her to regurgitate partly digested food for them, and also as a submission sign to dominant dogs. This face licking may be continued in their first home, to children especially. This behaviour should not be allowed and the puppy should be distracted by some other stimulus.

Shaking Hands

This is a submissive action, but one that is attractive and endearing, and it may well serve as a safety valve to the boisterous dog when visitors call. Teach the action, with suitable verbal cue, after the puppy has learnt to sit on command. You can teach older dogs new tricks too!

Inappropriate Eating Habits. Coprophagy

Some dogs begin in puppyhood to eat their own or their litter mates' solid excreta. If as tiny puppies their enclosure is not cleaned frequently, this behaviour may start, prompted from motives of investigation, play or possessiveness. In some species, notably rabbits and newborn foals, it is normal to eat the faeces of others, in order to acquire bacteria to aid the digestive process. The dog appears to find nothing repugnant about the performance, and perhaps this is a survival habit going back to pre-domestication. Not all dogs eat their own faeces, but it is not uncommon in young dogs. As the cause is not known, the cure will turn on trial and error.

1. Remove all faeces from the garden as soon as passed.
2. Keep close observation on the dog at all times. A dog with this problem should sleep in the owner's room as if left in the kitchen, there may be hardly any evidence that faeces have been passed and reconsumed. If the dog wakes you to go out in the night, at least you can prevent coprophagy becoming an established habit.

If caught in the act the dog should be firmly reprimanded (NO, or thrown object). Otherwise, the behaviour should be ignored and other remedies for the condition should be sought.

Suggestions which may be tried, one at a time:
1. Extra bran or vegetable fibre in the diet.

2. A change of diet to one which is slower to pass through the digestive tract, so leaving less edible residue. One of the biscuit-like complete diets based on soya-bean meal may suit.

3. The addition of vegetable oil or other fat to the diet so that the food remains longer in the stomach and is more completely digested.

4. The use of an enzyme powder on the food in case the diet is lacking in some necessary component. Your veterinary surgeon can supply this product.

5. If these remedies have failed, consult your veterinary surgeon, taking with you a note of what has been tried already, as well as details of the dog's feeding and vitamin regime.

Eating the Faeces of Other Animals

Dogs are attracted to eat the faeces of cats, cows, deer, rabbits, horses and other animals. They will also pay far too close attention to fields on which slurry has been spread as fertiliser.

This eating habit is entirely undesirable, as there is the possibility of transmission of disease, or worm eggs; the dog will almost certainly vomit at some time afterwards, and its breath will smell. It is very difficult on a country walk to prevent the dog discovering a pile of fresh horse manure while it is off the lead. NO said loudly as you see the dog's head go down, the thrown object if you are near enough, and calling the dog to you and praise-rewarding may be the answer, but most dogs will snatch a mouthful or two before they come running to you.

Prevention is the best method, dogs should always be lead across fields that have recently been inhabited by cows, and take care that their heads are held high by a short lead. The contents of cat litter trays should be disposed of efficiently so that the dog cannot exhume them.

Dogs will eat house plants, sometimes from sheer mischief, or else as a substitute for the grass which they would eat to some degree in the wild. Some houseplant leaves are poisonous, the Christmas Poinsettia being one of the most dangerous so these popular plants must never be left within a dog's reach. Cannabis plants are undesirable fodder too. If this urgent need for a grass-like substance occurs frequently, seek veterinary advice.

Dogs vomit easily, and some will bolt their food and bring it back undigested, only to eat it again with pleasure. We may feel revolted, but the dog seems to enjoy this action, which should be ignored unless the eating and vomiting cycle is frequent, when veterinary advice should be sought.

Window Dressing

Dogs which rampage at the window when other dogs are passing are territory guarding, sometimes much more fiercely than they would dare to do if they were able to confront the invader. It is an activity which breaks up the dog's inevitable boredom, and it is a matter for the owner to decide whether this "pleasure" to the dog should be allowed. If it is, clear the window sill to allow the dog easy access, as it is often those articles which are knocked down which eventually get destroyed. Some dogs which are destructive through boredom have been cured by constructing some kind of window seat where they can sit and watch passers-by thereby adding a great deal of interest to their day.

Hypersexuality in the Male Dog

We must recognise that to keep dogs singly within the boundaries of our own gardens, without sufficient exercise (few companion dogs get as much exercise as they are capable of taking), without the company of a canine pack and interaction with bitches is to keep them in an unnatural state. Domestication imposed a massive adaptation on the wild dog and modern conditions of living have imposed even more. We would not have it otherwise, for to let a dog run freely now is not only unkind but antisocial and against the law.

The male dog has had to modify its sexually orientated behaviour almost more than any other species and we have to realise that instinctive aggression towards other males, mounting behaviour, and territory marking have become the only expressions of sexuality left to the companion dog. Compulsive wandering, excitability and destructions are secondary mood expressions which may also be due to hyper- (excessive) sexuality in the companion dog but all these signs were only normal in its free-living ancestors.

Behaviour Demonstrations of Hypersexuality
1. Aggression.
2. Mounting other dogs, people, or inanimate objects.
3. Territory marking, especially urination about the house.
4. Roaming.
5. Destruction.
6. Excitability including excessive barking.

A recent survey taken among the owners of male dogs showed that well over half of their pets were performing some of the hypersexual behaviour patterns mentioned, very often at under twelve months old. This means that in the general dog population at least half are not a pleasure to own and they must be a source of embarrassment if not an actual liability to their owners. Few of the owners, in fact, complained of their dog's behaviour, taking these sexual expressions as part of the package deal of owning a male dog, and this may be the reason why bitches are by far the most popular choice of pet today, especially now that medication is available to control their seasons.

There can be little doubt that most of the traits which we term hypersexual are normal in male animals and it is merely a question of place, severity and frequency which makes this behaviour unacceptable. It is not really known what causes some males to be more sexually active than others but theoretically it could be the excessive production of male hormones or malfunction of those parts of the brain, the cerebral cortex, which controls sexual function. In many cases the undesirable behaviours are wholly or partly learnt and result from incorrect management by the owner. Poorly or inconsistently applied corrective measures in early life could be to blame and often such activities are promoted by unwitting reinforcement by the owner.

In the past the first consideration in cases of hyper-sexuality has been castration, but recent work has shown that this drastic measure, often very much resisted by *male owners*, is by no means uniformly effective.

Where dogs show mounting behaviour castration will be ineffective in about 30 per cent. of cases, it is only 50 per cent. effective in cases of territory marking (urination), in the house. Castration works in 60 per cent. of cases of fighting with other male dogs, but is no use at all in dogs which are aggressive towards people.

Castration is much more effective in the male cat than in the dog. The reason for the high failure rate for dog castration is that in many individuals the behaviour is not principally due to higher than normal hormonal levels. In some animals the centres in the brain seem to play a more important role and in these dogs castration will have little or no effect. In many instances it seems that hypersexual activities are learned and in these cases too castration will have little or no effect.

In recent years the use of female sex hormones to cancel the effect of the male hormone has been advocated and in many cases this seems to work better than castration, as the female hormones do seem to exert a calming effect on the brain so producing a good result in those dogs which are motivated by cerebral cortex activity. However the female hormone treatment does have to be administered continually or at least on a intermittent schedule, by tablets or by injection. It is suggested that the hormonal control be tried, after the behaviour control methods mentioned later have been applied, before turning to castration which may be of no use and is in any case irreversible. Your veterinary surgeon will be able to advise you.

Incidentally, it has been shown that the administration of a progestogen which is the synthetic female hormone component of the human contraceptive pill can be of use in training dogs. It seems that this hormone has a calmative effect, so if your dog is exhibiting severe signs of hyper-sexuality you should consider consulting your veterinary surgeon sooner, rather than later, as medication may help.

Behaviour Modification to Correct Hypersexuality Traits

Make sure you are not "encouraging" the dog by mild punishment, which may be construed as a reward. Mounting is a dominant behaviour so increase your leadership rôle and lower the dog's position in the hierarchy. If the dog is mounting specific objects, remove them. Petting and fondling should be avoided and food rewards substituted. Avoid exciting the dog by games but give sufficient walks. When the dog shows the slightest signs of beginning a sexual behaviour, distract it by throwing a ball, for instance, and then go on to give it a dominating training session. It is generally best to avoid all punishment in this regime as it will generally be ineffective and may lead to aggression, though the thrown object is useful where territory marking is excessive.

If the hypersexuality is a learned response the co-operation of all the family in the above regime should extinguish the behaviour. If the dog continues to be a problem in this way, see your veterinary surgeon.

Section VI

CHARACTERISTIC BEHAVIOUR

19

OLD AGE

THE life expectancy of dogs varies tremendously, being influenced by shape and breed, and by long-lived strains within that breed as the tendency to live beyond the average age is hereditary. Bulldogs are among the shortest lived of our dogs (seven to eight years), followed by the very large breeds (Danes and Mastiffs), and then by Boxers and Dobermans where a life span of ten to twelve years is a good average. In general, the smaller breeds tend to live longer and spaniels, small terriers and cross breds are among the longest lived dogs, fourteen to fifteen years being reached by many individuals and some going on until nearly twenty. It follows that Bulldogs are going into old age when cockers are just in their prime and Boxers, which remain puppies a long time, are just settling into reliable maturity. With advancing years dogs, like people, begin to suffer with problems associated with chronic diseases and degenerating body function but after many years of happiness with your dog you will not grudge the extra care and consideration it needs in old age.

Sight

The dog's sight degenerates with old age but also from a number of eye diseases to which the dog is prone, such as cataract. Blind or semi-blind dogs manage very well indeed on familiar territory, indeed you may not realise how little your ageing dog can see. When you realise its sight is failing, do not move the furniture around or leave hazards like wheelbarrows across the garden path. When you notice that your dog cannot see a ball or is bumping into things, get veterinary advice quickly. Ophthalmology is just one of the many areas of veterinary science which has made great strides forward in recent years.

A dog which tended in its youth to be aggressive with others may become more so when handicapped by failing sight, particularly when one eye is out of use and it can be taken by surprise from one side. You may have to keep such a dog on a lead in public parks.

Hearing

Some dogs become deaf with age but this matters relatively little as by the time your companion is deaf it will need few commands because it will be adjusted to doing what you want as a matter of habit. You may have to devise a system of hand signals, waving a white handkerchief will do, to attract the dog's attention from a distance. You will, of course, have a special care for blind and deaf dogs on roads and clifftop walks and in other hazardous situations, and you will take care not to let the dog be startled out of sleep.

Incontinence

Incontinence, or rather what the medical profession calls *frequency* becomes a problem in the ageing dog, which may find it impossible to go through a ten-hour night without passing urine. It is only in very old age, when the dog is failing that it will pass urine in its sleep, soiling its bed. You may find that you have to set up a routine similar to that of puppy days, either taking the dog into your room so that it can wake you when it needs to go out, or you can cover a small area of its sleeping quarters with newspaper which it can use. It is extremely unkind to withold water during the evening in the hope of keeping the dog dry at night and can be damaging to the kidneys. Before you accept that night frequency is due to ageing, do ask veterinary advice, since dogs suffer with cystitis and kidney problems, which may clear up quite quickly after treatment and your dog will then be back to "lasting all night" again. As the older dog will by now be immediately responsive to your wishes, it is little trouble to let it out to be clean frequently, saying your special code word. Some old dogs do not suffer from frequency, but when they do have to pass urine it has to be done as quickly as in puppy days; be ready to adjust to your old friend's needs and never, never blame because it cannot behave as it did in its prime.

Teeth

Some breeds lose their teeth quite early in life, Cavaliers and Yorkshire Terriers being among the earliest, at about six or seven years sometimes, but they can still manage quite hard biscuits. Very aged dogs may appreciate their food being put through a liquidiser to make a smooth consistency, tinned dog food is excellent this way.

An old dog can be given almost a new lease of life by the removal of decayed teeth and some attention to the gums and oral hygiene by a veterinary surgeon. Removal of pain, sometimes shown by drooping of the ear on the affected side, gives an added interest in eating and the dog becomes altogether more lively and, incidentally, much nicer to be near. It is a great pity to have to reject the advances of an old friend because of halitosis (bad breath), when a vet can do so much to cure the condition.

Indigestion

Reduced muscle tone in the intestine together with less inclination for exercise makes old dogs more prone to digestive troubles, and also to flatulence and "noises off" which may prove embarrassing in company. The larger breeds are especially inclined to producing tummy rumbles and obnoxious odours, and even worse, they have this awful way of walking away from the smell giving their owner reproachful glances as if to accuse *them* of defiling the atmosphere. There is little remedy but to laugh it off! It may pay to make a change in the diet, even a change in the brand of tinned meat can make a difference.

Arthritis

Arthritis is commonly seen in old dogs, but there is so much help which the vet can give them that the arthritic old dog is rather better off than a human sufferer from this condition. Dogs can take the pain relieving drugs which sometimes have to be denied to people because of long-term side effects. You may notice that the old dog grunts with pain as it gets up, and limps or staggers for the first few steps; that is the time to seek veterinary advice. If your dog has been covered by insurance for veterinary fees since its youth, the cover goes on until the end of its life, so that your dog can have all the benefits veterinary science has to offer to make it more comfortable. An ageing circulatory system makes the dog feel the cold more and it cannot move fast enough to keep warm. A short-coated dog may need a jacket to put on for its last trip into the garden at night in cold weather, get one that covers the chest as well as the back. Make the old dog's bed especially soft; you will notice that heavy breeds get callouses on elbows and hocks which can become very sore if the dog lies on a hard surface. The polystyrene-filled bean bags make excellent beds for arthritic dogs, providing warmth and support for aching joints. The arthritic dog must not be hurried, have patience while it gets out of its bed slowly to answer to your call. Take care not to bang into the dog not too steady on its feet when it first gets up and, above all, get veterinary advice to keep it pain free. Your friend may have several happy years with you yet.

Heart Disease

Heart Disease in dogs is usually shown by a chronic cough and an inability to take much exercise. Be suspicious of the dog which is no longer keen to run and sits down while it is out. Your veterinary surgeon can prescribe medication to support the heart's action which will help your dog.

Obesity

Middle-aged and old dogs tend to become fat. Excessive weight brings with it many problems, breathing difficulties, liver disease, intolerance of hot weather and skin troubles. Do not wait until your dog is old and overweight to think of slimming it down, it may then be too late because the body's metabolic rate slows down and the dog does not burn off so many calories by exercise. Prevention is better than cure, watch your dog's food intake in relation to its activity throughout life.

Management

If your management of your dog through puppy days, adolescence and adulthood has been good, perceptive and consistent there should be no need to talk of punishment in the dog's old age. Your dog will be living as you want it to and good behaviour will have become a habit. Old age is the time for indulgences and pampering, even perhaps letting the dog dominate you just a little. The matriarchal Boxer, Pooka, at eleven years old is demanding, autocratic, has us jumping at her every bark, thrives on privileges the other dogs do not get and we would not have her any other way. The cleverness of old dogs is something to be enjoyed, it is a very special attribute of their later years.

20

DISEASE

BECAUSE you are so familiar with the behaviour patterns of your dog you will have the advantage of knowing when those patterns change from the normal *for your dog* and so you may be able to recognise the onset of a disease before overt signs show. It is as well to bear in mind that dogs will behave differently when they are feeling unwell or have pain, so that instead of trying to modify these behaviours by remedial techniques you seek veterinary advice early. You will then spare your dog a lot of suffering and misunderstanding and will have a much greater chance of getting the condition cleared up quickly.

Aggression

Sudden aggression in a normally placid dog may have its origin in *pain*, possibly an abscess forming, impacted anal glands, chronic ear conditions or toothache. Brain disorders associated with epilepsy, infectious disease and tumours may cause dogs to become unnaturally aggressive. It is always wise to seek veterinary attention if a normally pleasant pet shows sudden bouts of bad temper. Try to work out any associated factors which may help the vet in his diagnosis.

Hyperactivity

Dogs with a mild degree of over-activity of the thyroid gland (hyperthyroidism), may become nervous and irritable as well as over-active and the problem may become extended into a hyperkinetic state, characterised by extreme restlessness. If you have a too active dog, be sure that its behaviour is not being encouraged and reinforced, especially by children. If you cannot identify the cause of the behaviour, consult your vet.

Hallucinations

Some dogs develop a behaviour pattern of standing or sitting and looking at imaginary objects, they may even stare at and try to catch non-existent flies, or attack the ground for no discernable reason. The cause of this bizarre behaviour is not known but it may arise from visual defects or from malfunctions of the brain. Veterinary advice should be sought for searching examination of the probable cause. It must always be remembered that such behaviours may be partially learnt and continued because the dog receives attention and therefore inadvertent reward when it carries out this weird action. The behaviour should be ignored and it may be possible to extinguish it in this way but because the tendency to inappropriate behaviour of this kind is an abnormality which could be inherited, such dogs should not be used for breeding.

Dobermans sometimes engage in an activity called "flank sucking" in which they grasp their loins in their mouths and stay in that position for long periods. The cause is not known and no effective treatment has been devised. Some dogs suck at their paws and pull lumps out of their coats, even destroying themselves down to the flesh and causing wounds which are very difficult to heal. The cause may have been originally one of irritation or a foreign body, but like children picking at spots, the dog goes on working at the site as a means of relieving tension or boredom. Veterinary help will be needed to institute some regime of medication to induce the dog to leave the area alone so that healing can begin or the original cause can be corrected. You may also be shown how to bandage a different part of the dog's body so that its attention is diverted.

Coma

Diabetes, liver disease, inflammation of the kidneys and abnormal levels of essential minerals in the blood can lead to coma, or to hyper-excitability. Such dramatic changes in behaviour require professional help so that the exact cause can be established and the appropriate treatment given.

21
NORMAL BODILY FUNCTION

The Bitch

Bitch owners should be prepared for the changes which affect temperament to a greater or lesser degree during the hormonal cycle (the season and subsequent false pregnancy and nursing). Each bitch varies in the way this time affects her, she may become more excitable and demanding, or more lethargic, may refuse to eat, or may be short-tempered and more dominant, but the changes are usually minimal and should be accepted as far as possible.

If the behaviour is very much exaggerated and the bitch tends to become very dominant at this time then there is a good case for controlling the heat either surgically or medically. These changes are not learned, so they do not lend themselves to behaviour modification techniques.

False Pregnancy and Nursing Behaviour

This has been described previously; in each bitch it will vary in intensity, and this behaviour too cannot be modified by our techniques, as it is compulsive in the bitch which believes that she actually has puppies to nurse and protect. If the bitch or her owner feels real distress, then medication can be used to control the milk production and also the nervous signs. An experience of false pregnancy as intense as this is a good case for neutering the bitch, or controlling the season by the newer medical method, otherwise she is likely to suffer in the same way after every season all her life.

Maternal Behaviour

Maternal behaviour is instinctive and not learnt, so it cannot be altered by behaviour modification techniques. Aggressive protection of the puppies can be aggravated if the bitch feels threatened by other animals or unfamiliar humans approaching her puppies too closely. As with every other attribute, bitches vary in the strength of their maternal possessiveness; some will allow other bitches, usually their mothers or sisters living in the same household, to lie with them and help take care of their puppies. Others will guard so intensely and be so busy warding off real or imaginary threats that they will fail to nurse their puppies adequately. It makes sense for the owner to arrange that the newly whelped bitch is kept in seclusion from human and animal visitors for the first two to two-and-a-half weeks after the birth. In kennels it is not unknown for one bitch to invade the nest of another and kill all the puppies. The aggressor very often has a similar aged litter of her own, so nursing bitches must not be kept within earshot of another litter, as the noise of other puppies seems to excite bitches unreasonably.

Some bitches are very particular about which of the human pack may attend to their puppies, and they may make aggressive moves towards a visiting veterinary surgeon at this time. Although owners would like a photographic record of the litter, the presence of a photographer often excites and upsets the bitch. All handling of nursing bitches should be as tactful as possible to avoid upsetting the bitch at this sensitive time, and it should not be assumed that, because a bitch is normally friendly with some human or dog, she will allow them to approach her when she has puppies.

Conversely, some bitches lack maternal instinct to greater or lesser degree; some are easily distracted away from their puppies and the extreme condition is unwilling-ness to pay the puppies any attention and not even to be willing to stay in a bed with them. The latter condition may have some painful cause, either the bitch has a con-dition of the uterus which is making her feel ill, or perhaps the nipples are too sore to allow the puppies to feed. The remedy may be as simple as cutting the puppies' nails, scratching the teat area can be very painful to the bitch. Because good mothering behaviour is essential to the sur-vival of the offspring it is important that breeders do not use bitches with either of the extremes of maternal behaviour described, however closely such bitches may, in external appearance, approach the ideal for the breed.

Conclusion

In the space of this small book it has not been possible to cover all the inappropriate behaviours that may occur in dogs but we hope that we have succeeded in giving enough help to owners and prospective owners of dogs so that they may apply our principle to their own particular difficulties. If you are in doubt or find that the techniques which we advise do not work, even when you apply them with diligence and co-operation of everyone in contact with the dog, then seek professional advice without delay. Do not be afraid to turn to your vet for help, he should be your friend and counsellor on all matters appertaining to your pets.

Our ultimate aim is to help you to make each puppy and dog you acquire into a successful companion which will be in your home for the whole of its life. If, by writing this book, we can do something to alleviate the enormous numbers of pet animals which are discarded and eventually destroyed every year, we shall feel it was all worthwhile.

If you follow the management techniques described with patience, perseverance and perception, you will have a dog which is a pleasure to own, a dog that will be admired and envied by all your friends.

Jim Evans, owner, with his wife, of Anna, the Doberman, knows that you will say with truth "My Dog is Better than Your Dog!" Kay White, owner of Pooka, Berry, and several other Boxers, and Harold White, owner of Tigger, know you will get as much pleasure and fun as we have had from all the dogs which have lived with us.

APPENDIX

Useful Addresses

The Kennel Club, 1 Clarges Street, London, W1.

Weekly Newspapers: *Dog World*, 9 Tufton Street, Ashford, Kent TN23 1QN.
Our Dogs, 5 Oxford Road, Station Approach, Manchester M60 1SX.

Dog Breeders' Associates, c/o Mrs S. Blumire, 1 Abbey Road, Bourne End, Bucks. Tel.: Bourne End 20943. Circulates lists of puppies for sale. No charge to buyers.

PetPlan Ltd. All types of dog insurance, including for veterinary fees, and cover for puppies 6–12 weeks. 319–327 Chiswick High Road, London W4 4HH. Tel.: 01-995 1414.

British Veterinary Association: 7 Mansfield Street, London W1M 0AT. Tel.: 01-636 6541

YOUR DOG'S PARTICULARS

Name	Breeder's name and address
Date of birth	Veterinary Surgeon's name and address
Breed	
Colour	Surgery hours Telephone
Sex	Boarding kennel Address
Insurance Policy No.	Telephone

Fig. 17. Your dog's particulars.

INDEX